A NEW MORAL ORDER

A NEW MORAL ORDER
*Studies in Development Ethics
and Liberation Theology*

DENIS GOULET
Center for the
Study of Development and Social Change

With a foreword by Paulo Freire

Orbis Books
Maryknoll, New York
1974

To my father

Contents

Acknowledgments

The ideas contained in this book were first presented at the Ezra Squier Tipple Lectures, Drew University, New Jersey, November 13–16, 1972. I thank Charles Courtney for his invitation and his sustained interest in the ethics of development.

Orlando Fals-Borda's careful review of the chapter on his work prevented several errors of fact. Although he voiced his opinions clearly, he scrupulously respected the autonomy of my interpretative statements. I received a valuable critique of L.J. Lebret's work from Floreal Forni. Interviews with Gonzalo Arroyo and Gustavo Gutierrez helped me revise chapters 4 and 5. My thanks also to Jacques Chonchol and Dom Helder Camara for generously making time available whenever I have visited Chile or Brazil.

I am grateful to Atheneum Publishers for permitting the adaptation of materials now incorporated into chapter 1.

None of the persons mentioned, however, can be blamed for the final product, responsibility for which must rest on my own shoulders.

Foreword

It was in Santiago that I first met Denis Goulet. He
was introduced to me, in 1966, by Antonio Baltar, a
Brazilian urban strategist and United Nations expert
working in Chile, who, like Goulet, was a close friend
of L.J.Lebret. Baltar not only introduced us; years
earlier, in northeast Brazil, he had been the first person
to tell me of Goulet's work and his concern with the
ethical aspects of development.

The first moments of that conversation, which lasted
long into the night, were sufficient for me to recognize
that I had before me a sensitive and intellectually challenging man who had to be taken seriously. He did not
speak to me of the Third World and its problems as
a falsely impartial analyst who remains cold and aloof,
who wears gloves and a white apron as he dissects in
an antiseptic room. Neither did he come across as a
shrewd helper or a narrow-minded bureaucrat. On the
contrary, he spoke to me as a man who was deeply
involved in the drama of that world to which he felt
committed. Furthermore, he did not try to parlay his
own vivid experiences within the world of dependency
and silence into a form of revolutionary safe-conduct
which would open new doors for him in Latin America.

He spoke with humility, and this added great weight to his words.

Goulet did not then view the Third World—nor does he view it now—as a mere object about which one could become expert without simultaneously assuming that world and being assumed by it. I think it is important to stress this, lest Goulet's relentless probing into ethical considerations be mistaken for the metaphysical ravings of a philosopher masking his interest in preserving the status quo. On the contrary, Goulet is a restless man who never ceases to look at life with a permanent sense of astonishment, whose ethical preoccupations are born of communion with the silent regions of the world, with the "wretched of the earth." It is to these groups, in their very character as dominated classes, and to their authentic leaders that falls the historic task—and this I wish to emphasize—of overcoming their economic, political, social, and cultural dependence, which accounts for their being the "wretched of the earth."

To overcome this situation—which cannot be done without radical transformation of the class society—requires the taking of a prophetic position, as I understand it. This is the prophetic position which is described and referred to by Goulet in his book; the individuals of whom he writes have tried, or are now trying, to assume such a position.

In reality, no mere reformism—bourgeois or proletarian—can bring about this radical triumph over the situation of dependency. Bourgeois reformism does not extend any further than the modernization of a dependent society; moreover, it helps to preserve the subordinate character of that entire society as well as the power of the dominating classes. In turn, thanks to its fundamental ambiguity, proletarian reformism is either crushed in the very process of struggling for radical change, or it declines into mere revolutionary assistance, in which the party fears losing the masses, even though it grants them a limited amount of political participation.

Bourgeois reformism is the answer given by the dominating classes when their commitment to the ideology of modernization is challenged and the contradictions within the heart of their society become exacerbated.

Proletarian reformism is an ideological distortion of the revolution, which, under these circumstances, is emptied of meaning.

The first of these two reformisms opens the way to populism, the second to bureaucratic rigidity.

Accordingly, neither of these two modes of reformism has anything to do with a position of authentic prophecy. And authentic prophecy cannot be achieved in the absence of a dialectic unity between denunciation of the oppressive reality and annunciation of a new reality, which will give birth to a new man and a new woman. This merger of denouncing with announcing is what establishes the revolutionary praxis of the dominated classes in union with their leaders.

Since all true prophecy is concretely and critically utopian, it is necessarily laden with hope, although it never falls into alienation or wishful thinking. Hence, there is no prophecy worthy of the name when there is an idealist's or subjectivist's pose or, on the other hand, a mechanistic posture of objectivity.

For the prophet it is not enough merely to speak in the name of those who cannot speak: he or she must make a commitment to the cause of those who have no voice. The prophet struggles along with them so that all of them may speak.

It would be sheer naïveté to nourish the hope that bourgeois reformism, which obviously serves the dominators, could extend to the dominated the opportunity of assuming the attitudes of a "class for itself." On the contrary, it is of the very nature of this reformism to strive to hinder by whatever means, the raising of class-consciousness amid the dominated classes. The dominating class, in fact, does not commit suicide.

Just as it fights against bourgeois reformism, authentic prophecy likewise does battle against the ideological distortion which results in proletarian reformism, although it laments having to do so.

In agreeing to write a few words of prologue to this book, which I judge to be truly excellent for many reasons, I did not intend to analyze or dissect it in its various stages. That is not my style of writing prologues.

My intention is solely this: without further ado, to invite the reader to enter into contact with Goulet's thought and with the hope of which he writes.

Paulo Freire
Geneva, 1973

Chapter I

ETHICS IN DEVELOPMENT

Most books on development or technical assistance contain resounding declarations about a better life for all, greater equity in the distribution of wealth, and the need for partnership between developed and underdeveloped nations, classes, and societies. Underlying all such statements is some ethic, usually implicit, of progress, of social justice, of equality, and of human solidarity in the fight against misery.

Development Ethics:
A Discipline in the Making

The French writer Julien Benda was once asked by a journalist to define existentialism as a philosophy. He replied, only half-facetiously, "There is no such thing as existentialism; there are only existentialists." I am tempted to apply his provocative answer to the ethics of development. Clearly, there is no preexisting discipline bearing that name. And very few scholars have made the value-laden, ethical questions posed by development the central object of their study. Hence one looks in vain for a body of literature treating development's ethical issues *ex professo.* This is a marked contrast to the volumes written on the disciplines of political, economic, social, and administrative development. In addition a host of scholars from other disciplines—anthropologists, social psychologists, planners, geographers, demographers, statisticians, and the like—write copiously about development and underdevelopment from their own vantage points. Many of these authors discuss values and the ethics of social change, but they never place them at the heart of their analysis. For them ethical concerns remain mere corollaries of substantive work done under other lights.

A few illustrations may prove helpful. Gunnar Myrdal (particularly in *Asian Drama* and *Objectivity in Social Research*) openly declares the values which preside over his monumental studies of the "vicious circle" of underdevelopment. Writers such as Kenneth Boulding *(The Meaning of the Twentieth Century)*, Robert Heilbroner *(The Great Ascent)*, Barbara Ward *(The Lopsided World)*, John Kenneth Galbraith *(The New Industrial State)*, and Robert Theobald *(The Rich and the Poor)* do bring an explicit moral vision to their interpretation of development and industrialization. Yet even these authors fail to analyze underdevelopment primarily in ethical terms. That is, they do not systematically define the symbolic and institutional requirements of the good life, of the just society excluding domination and exploitation in a world of convulsive technological changes.

Perhaps the closest approach to a genuine ethics of development can be found in certain French writers: François Perroux, L.J. Lebret, Jacques Austruy, Jean-Marie Albertini, Henri Desroches, Destanne de Bernis, Pierre George, and others. Yet they too are specialists in other disciplines, who enrich their studies with ethical categories largely extrinsic to the dynamism of their empirical analysis. By citing writers of the French school I do not wish to imply that United States development scholars have ignored ethical issues. On the contrary, social scientists such as Edward Banfield *(The Moral Basis of a Backward Society)*, David Apter *(The Politics of Modernization)*, Lloyd and Susanne Rudolph *(The Modernity of Tradition)*, Irving Louis Horowitz *(Three Worlds of Development)*, and Albert O. Hirschman *(Journeys Toward Progress)* are often quite concerned with ethical questions. Nevertheless, like the French writers just named, they borrow their basic theoretical concepts and methodological tools from some other discipline. This is why their handling of development's ethical issues often remains tangential, incidental, or speculative.

An important stream of Third World writers now stress such categories as imperialism, domination, and dependency. They appeal to a sense of ethical outrage as they condemn the economic exploitation or cultural invasion practiced by the developed on the underdeveloped. Nevertheless, their analytical tools are usually those of conventional specialized disciplines, broadened and invigorated by a conscious commitment to the Marxist dialectic of history. Examples of such authors are Fernando Enrique Cardoso, Pierre Jallée, E. Falleto, Theotonio dos Santos, Samir Amin, J.J. Hernandez Arregui, and Alvaro Vieira Pinto.

One finds still another kind of quasi-ethical development literature: the proliferating theological reflections on underdevelopment, liberation, and foreign aid as these affect mission enterprises in the Third World, the social concern of churches, and the redefinition of religious commitment to historical tasks. Among those who have written on development from this viewpoint are Gabriel Bowe, Charles Elliott, Gustavo Gutierrez, Dom Helder Camara, Stephen Rose, Ivan Illich, Arend van Leeuwen, and Richard Shaull.

In sum, the ethics of development is an infant discipline. Recent efforts to articulate a properly ethical theory and method for studying development are, of necessity, embryonic. The work of the late L.J. Lebret has greatly influenced my own efforts in this field.[1] In a later chapter I shall examine in detail his innovations in interdisciplinary research and planning. Here I need only reiterate the point he made insistently: the links between economic *science* and moral *philosophy* must be restored.

Indeed the development problem resurrects, in a new mode, the most ancient ethical questions: what is the good life, what is the just society, what stance should societies take *vis-à-vis* the forces of nature and of technology or artificial nature? The new mode derives from traits peculiar to the twentieth-century world: the enormous scale of operations, technical complexities, multiple interdependencies among systems and component units of systems, and the ever-shortening time lag between the impingement of disturbing social stimuli and the deadline for an adequate response. More than anything else, however, it is the very bankruptcy of conventional wisdom on development which summons moral philosophy to a rebirth.

The Rebirth of Moral Philosophy

Modern moral philosophy is proving unable to answer ethical questions raised by development. According to David Apter, a political scientist, the study of modernization "brings us back to the search for first principles, and rapid-fire developments in social theory and the breakthroughs in the biological sciences, not to speak of the retreat of philosophy into linguistics, have combined to render us philosophically defenseless and muddled."[2]

It was not always thus, for moral philosophy is one of the ancestors of economics. Only gradually did economics gain autonomy as a separate branch of learning. Plato, in his ethical system, discussed but one properly economic question: the division of labor. For him that was simply an aspect of justice. In the words of economist George Wilson, Plato held that "each man should get enough, and no more, to enable him to perform the function that fate or the special educational system Plato

The material contained in this section originally appeared in a different version in the *The Cruel Choice*, by Denis Goulet. Copyright 1971 by Denis Goulet. Reprinted by arrangement with Atheneum Publishers.

outlines had chosen him to perform within the confines of the polis."[3] Like Plato, Aristotle endorsed Socrates' position that "to have few wants is godlike."

With hindsight, many regard this restraint as a rationalization for the static gross product of the Greek city-states, which operated at low economic levels. Perhaps, however, it was nothing more than an early example of a tendency often displayed by philosophy—the disposition to become, in the words of two modern authors, the "handmaiden ready to provide a beautiful prospectus for a house of habit and custom in which society has long since been comfortably adjusting its goods and chattels."[4]

The Greek outlook on the division of labor and the accumulation of wealth prevailed in European thought until the advent of medieval scholasticism. By the thirteenth century, inquiry into the satisfaction of human wants had become part of a holistic theological system. Certainly, medieval theologians and philosophers did not rely upon Greek wisdom as their only source of inspiration. On the contrary, their inherited tradition had "baptized" that wisdom in Christian waters. The central tenets of early Christian ethics as applied to economic life were the existence of hierarchy and order in society, the providential origin of the individual's appointed station in life, and the obligation incumbent upon all to practice distributive as well as commutative justice. Centuries later, Albert the Great, Thomas Aquinas, and Antoninus of Florence elaborated guidelines to be obeyed by merchants, craftsmen, and noblemen in setting just prices, assessing taxes, determining proper lending practices, and making proper use of superfluous goods. They stressed the ancient patristic doctrine of the common destination of the earth's goods—to meet the needs of all men. They relied heavily on early texts, such as this one from Chrysostom:

> Everything comes from the earth, we all come from a single man, we all have the same sojourn [here on earth]. There are things which are common, such as baths, cities, public squares and promenades. Now you will notice that with regard to goods such as these, there is no dispute and peace is complete. But if, on the other hand, someone should attempt to usurp or appropriate a good to himself, quarrels immediately arise. It is as though nature itself revolted against men's attempt to divide things which God himself had united. This is the result of our efforts when we seek to have goods of our own, when we mouth these two insipid words "yours and mine." Remove these words, let us have no more quarrels, no more enmities .... The community [of goods] is far more suitable to us and is better grounded in nature than [private] property. God has given us the first goods in common so that we should know how to place the second kind in common.[5]

For several centuries thereafter, Europe professed doctrines that had been formulated in a feudal setting which was characterized by little trade beyond neighboring manors, innumerable units of exchange and measurement, and, more important, generalized economic stagnation at low levels. The Biblical doctrine of stewardship continued to influence the morality of economic life. Long after mercantilists, physiocrats, and other theorists of "political arithmetic" (as knowledge about wealth had come to be called) began discussing new doctrines, men found it hard to conceive of land, labor, and capital as abstract factors in a process whose overt aim was to produce wealth. Work and the accumulation of wealth had not yet become proper subjects for independent analysis. The idea of the propriety (not to say the necessity) of a system organized on the basis of *personal gain* had not yet taken root. Neither had a self-contained economic world emerged separated from its moral context. Robert Heilbroner illustrates contemporary practices before profit-seeking had obtained social legitimacy by citing the trial of Robert Keane, of Boston, in 1644. Keane, a minister of the gospel, was charged with a heinous crime: he had earned over sixpence profit on the shilling, an outrageous gain! The court debated whether to excommunicate him for his sin, but in view of his spotless past it dismissed him with a fine of 200 pounds. On the following Sunday the local minister denounced "some false principles of trade," among them:

> I. That a man might sell as dear as he can, and buy as cheap as he can.
> II. If a man lose by casualty of sea, etc., in some of his commodities, he may raise the price of the rest.
> III. That he may sell as he bought, though he paid too dear. . . . All false, false, false, cries the minister; to seek riches for riches' sake is to fall into the sin of avarice [6]

By the seventeenth century, of course, commerce had already acquired new dimensions and new legitimacy in daily practice. Industry had begun to harness mechanical inventions to tasks of production, to concentrate a labor force, to abide by the law of capital accumulation, and to adjust itself to the demands of what was becoming a competitive market. *Homo oeconomicus* now existed; all he needed was a doctrine to explain him.

In 1776 a rambling, encyclopedic work was published by Adam Smith, a man of leisure who had abandoned a university career as professor of moral philosophy. *The Wealth of Nations* was, in effect, the Declaration of Independence severing economics from moral philosophy; with its publication, economics became a separate discipline. Rapidly, however, "Smith's followers lost sight of the fundamentally moral nature of human action. So much so that in atomizing economics they were led to object to Smith's introducing social dimensions into the economic domain. Smith's separations had been provisional; the systematic, methodical, and strictly deductive approach was the work of his followers."[7] The author of *The Wealth of Nations*, a treatise on man's propensity to barter for gain, was also the moral philosopher whose *Theory of Moral Sentiments* defended the sentiment of sympathy as holding society together. For Adam Smith these two propensities were not in conflict, since both were governed by the higher regulative principle of justice; the "invisible hand" that guided society was not a cynical apology for immoral economics, but an expression of the author's unshakable belief in divine providence. Nevertheless, Smith had given a powerful thrust to the separation of economics from the larger context of moral life. And long before 1776 "the equation between private vice and public virtue had become commonplace."[8]

The great economists after Smith—Ricardo, Mill, Malthus, Marx, Jevons, Marshall, Keynes—remained moral reformers at heart, directing their analysis toward contemporary problems. But now that economics had acquired a life of its own, neither ethics nor theology provided norms or direction.[9] Even Marx, a passionate moral critic in *The Communist Manifesto*, remained utterly detached from considerations of morality in *Das Kapital*. In Heilbroner's words:

> The book describes with fury, but it analyzes with cold logic. For what Marx has set for his goal is to discover the intrinsic tendencies of the capitalist system, its inner laws of motion, and in so doing, he has eschewed the easy but less convincing means of merely expatiating on its manifest shortcomings.[10]

Marx's very style, even more than Mill's, reveals how deep the chasm between ethics and economics had grown. The subsequent history of both disciplines has widened the gap. In the distant past, economic doctrines were almost always associated with moral codes about the manner of work and the division of the product. Today, on the contrary, economics has become the most abstractly mathematical and the most practically applicable of all the social sciences. It has achieved great virtuosity in handling means, but it is no longer competent to evaluate ends or ideals.

Nevertheless, the new teleological questions posed by development have reawakened economists to their long-forgotten intellectual kinship with moral philosophers. As early as 1954 Adolf Berle wrote:

> that the really great corporation managements have

reached a position for the first time in their history in which they must consciously take account of philosophical considerations. They must consider the kind of a community in which they have faith, and which they will serve, and which they intend to help construct and maintain. In a word, they must consider at least in its more elementary phases the ancient problem of the "good life" and how their operations in a community can be adapted to affording or fostering it.[11]

Or as Galbraith put it, in 1962, "the final requirement of modern development planning is that it have a theory of consumption.... *More important, what kind of consumption should be planned?*"[12]

Economics seems to have come full circle from finding a rationale for a small and static economic surplus, a situation which led men to disdain most forms of the accumulation of wealth and to emphasize just distribution. Now there is a new concern for economic surplus, which is leading some economists to deemphasize growth, to study the composition and distribution of the gross national product, and, more broadly, to consider the quality of our wants. Economic growth doubtless remains the first order of business in much of the world, even within significant portions of affluent society. Nonetheless, economic discipline itself is once again raising teleological questions long considered the special province of philosophy. The United Nations Conference on the Human Environment (Stockholm, 1972), the debate generated by Meadows' *The Limits of Growth*, and the appearance of competing models for world futures have all brought new urgency to the value dimensions of basic development decisions. But nothing has equipped economic science to answer its own

questions, so, more and more, economics looks to
ethics. But ever since the separation of economics
from the study of morals, ethics has had a dismal
career. It, too, is presently incapable of answering
development's normative questions.

Why is modern ethics so ill-prepared? The eman-
cipation of economics from moral philosophy was
simply one manifestation of a general trend toward
specialization in knowledge. Major gains were
made in those branches of learning which became
cumulative by relying on empirical investigation
derived from revisable and nondeductible theories.
The greatest methodological progress came in the
natural sciences. Such progress greatly facilitated
observation and classification and was the spring-
board for major breakthroughs in theory (in
biology, physics, astronomy). Later, borrowing
freely from the natural sciences, the "sciences of
man" also reached impressive levels of generality
in the theoretical order (systems theory, general
theory of action). The social sciences deal with life,
however, and even recent gains have not dis-
sipated the growing malaise of social scientists in
the face of life's complexities.

In turn, ethics, stripped of its effective role as
the setter of society's norms, strayed along diverse
paths. Soon all philosophies gradually fell into dis-
repute. With the success of the experimental
method and the rising ascendancy of empirical science, philosophical speculation came to be
regarded as an armchair procedure of dubious value.[13] In a recent essay Ernest Gellner speculated
with irony "that if the several thousands or more
of professional philosophers in America were all
assembled in one place and a small nuclear device

were detonated over them, American society would remain totally unaffected.... There would be no gap, no vacuum, in the intellectual economy that would require plugging."[14]

Many modern philosophers have taken highly individualistic, existentialist routes, a jungle maze replete with meandering byways. Others have embraced Marxist prescriptive doctrine and become exegetes of the new scripture of dialectical materialism. A third group, few in number and limited in influence, maintains allegiance to natural-law morality.

In developed countries, however, most ethical theorists have chosen the road of positivism. And mainstream positivist ethics has abandoned normative prescription on the grounds that it is pretentious, unscientific, or both. Instead, ethics now seeks to derive guidelines for action from social preferences, positive law, psychological conditioning, or the demands of efficiency. By its own admission, positivist ethics regards teleology as meaningless. Therefore, when economists ask what consumption is for, or what kinds of goods foster the good life, or what is the nature of welfare, positivist ethics has nothing to say.

Marxist ethics does supply one set of answers to these questions. But, as its own spokesmen acknowledge today, Marxist ethics has long been under the spell of its own dogma and has refused to examine a whole gamut of profoundly meaningful questions on the grounds that such questions are vestiges of "bourgeois decadence."[15] Only in recent years have certain Marxist moralists begun to view ethical inquiry as an essentially open-ended process without predetermined answers.

Existentialists, for their part, have either
rejected social ethics as unimportant or engaged
in tortuous, self-analyzing (and self-justifying)
efforts to build dialectical bridges from personal
freedom as the ultimate value to the demands of
social philosophy. Such quasi-absolute commitment to personal freedom necessarily renders the
formulation of a social ethic difficult. Nevertheless,
Camus and (in more explicitly critical terms)
Sartre have laid a foundation for bridging the distance between personal and societal ethics. Yet
their language and style are so strongly conditioned by their personal experiences of World
War II and post-war France that it has been difficult for underdeveloped countries to accept their
social morality.[16]

This explains why many Latin American social
philosophers find Marxism far more attractive
than existentialism. For one Brazilian philosopher, "The philosophy of existence, among all contemporary doctrines, is the one which most clearly
exposes its followers to the danger of alienation."
He believes the reason is that "existential
philosophy is the philosophy of the centers of domination over underdeveloped regions."[17]

In short, development economists do not receive
much normative help from moral philosophers
even when they seek it. On issues of importance
to policy makers and development planners, the
available ethical systems provide little light. Existentialists are too individualistic and too complex,
Marxists too deductively prescriptive and not suf-
ficiently responsive to social and symbolic
relativities.[18] Natural-law moralists are increasingly viewed as defenders of a particular confes-

sional doctrine in a world becoming increasingly secular and pluralistic. Positivists suffer from an overdose of success in description and analysis, which has caused atrophy of their ability to engage in normative or evaluative inquiry. To put it bluntly, the mainstream of moral philosophy has run dry.

Nevertheless, as Etienne Gilson remarks, "the first law to be inferred from philosophical experience is: Philosophy always buries its undertakers"[19] For over twenty-five centuries the death of philosophy has been regularly attended by its revival. The present moribund state of moral philosophy may be the harbinger of a new spring. Few modern philosophical systems attempt to provide a total explanation of reality. The reason, in part, is that philosophers know how difficult it is to reach a synthesis of realities which are themselves fluid and complex. Continual inquiry into meaning goes on, nonetheless, and we may soon witness the birth of new philosophies whose hallmarks are nondogmatism, a reaction against simplistic forms of relativity, and a genuinely self-critical spirit.

There is an "economic" law at work here. Human societies cannot long endure unless their need for meaning is met by adequate philosophies. Technology and the effects of mass demonstrations presently challenge the values of all societies. United Nations documents, development plans, and aid manifestos talk about a "better life," "greater equity in the distribution of wealth," "the need to assure social improvement for all." Here is clear proof of the existence of a "demand" for development ethics. It is the "supply" side which is wanting. If moral philosophers prove incapable of supplying answers, or if they take refuge in concepts alien to the real experiences which alone can provide raw materials for reflection, others—economists, anthropologists, sociologists, psychologists —will try to formulate an ethics of development. But from where will they draw the wisdom? Neither economics *qua* economics, nor anthropology *qua* anthropology can bring normative unity and value synthesis to the complex human experience of development.

A far more alarming possibility, of course, is that political demagogues, technological manipulators, or the high priests of ideological thought control will make the attempt. Notwithstanding the lateness of the hour, there may still be time for moral philosophers to stop "moralizing" and undertake serious analysis of the ethical problems posed by development, underdevelopment, and planning. In order to succeed, they must go to the factory with Simone Weil or to the market place with Eric Weill. Better still, they must go to the planning board and the irrigation project.

A full inquiry into why moral philosophy has become impotent to deal with economic issues would perforce include a critique of Christian morality, the ethical matrix out of which the developed world has confronted the Third World. Twentieth-century men are fully conscious of the "mystification" wrought by moral values in the past. They know the long history wherein developed societies have used these values as a cover for the defense of their interests. In the light of such history, one is understandably skeptical about any development ethics. Even Marx's radical unmasking of the class nature of all morality leaves us doubting; at best the universal claims of the class morality he proposes in its stead enjoy dubious applicability to a rapidly changing technological milieu. Neither events nor its own evolution inspire much confidence in the ability of Marxist moral theory to avoid substituting voluntarism for wisdom.

Although we stand in urgent need of a "reconstruction of social ethics," no single mind can effect such a reconstruction. As Thomas Kuhn argues so persuasively in *The Structure of Scientific Revolutions*, intellectual breakthroughs are rarely the creation of isolated individuals.[20] On the contrary, new knowledge gestates in living communities engaged in active dialogue, the symbolic significance of which must be deciphered and recodified. Reality forces today's moralists to renounce pretensions at grand theory. Paradoxically, however, they must learn to think in new experiential and empirical modes without becoming ashamed of speaking prescriptively. At best their prescriptions will have relative merit, and they must be tested. Moralists may—indeed, they must—aspire to universality, not some ready-made universality, but *a tentative model of partial universality in the making*. Through examination of the very processes by which societies give different responses to the stimuli provided by technology, planning, the quest for new meaning, and alternative value systems, a normative system must emerge. Like every system, it will be ephemeral. But moralists must learn to glory in the ephemeral without abdicating their passion for the normative.

The reflections of any man, or any team of men, always carry the brand of ethnocentrism. Full lib-

eration from ethnocentrism is impossible.
Whatever be his formal intent, his cross-cultural
sensitivity, or his sophisticated use of protective
devices to safeguard objectivity, any philosopher
or social scientist will propound truths derived
from limited, personal, cognitive experience in a
given cultural mode. If he is North American, he
cannot speak for Africans or the Chinese. If he
is Indian, he cannot speak for Arabs. Nevertheless,
he might possibly—in his best moments of sublime,
flashing intuitions—manage to speak as a man.
Strip away his Western accent, his African cos-
tume, his Asian formula, and you may have something which can become universal. Literature
supplies us with examples of great writers who
have initiated their readers to the universal by
plunging deeply into the particular reality they
knew best. Shakespeare is so very English, but
he has plucked heart strings outside the British
Empire. So with Lao-Tze; his masterful essay on
The Way is thoroughly rooted in Chinese sensibil-
ity, yet it strikes a responsive chord in African
and Western minds. And Dante, so profoundly
Italian, has won rightful acclaim as a universal
genius. Ideally, it should be thus for moral
philosophers who address themselves to the ethics
of development. Authors will be culture-bound,
but, if they are successful, they will attain a regis-
ter of expression wherein values are *capable of
becoming universal.*

The prospective development moralist faces four
tasks:

• He must elaborate a consciously critical position
on the goals of development.
• He must analyze development processes from the

inside and isolate (as a chemist isolates an element in a compound) the values and countervalues latent in those processes.

• He must prepare guidelines for different behavioral sectors which are of crucial importance to development processes. These guidelines will constitute, in embryonic form, normative strategies to be followed in a variety of areas.

• Most important, he must build a coherent theoretical framework in which partial and fragmentary ethical constructs can be unified around a few central, interrelated analytical concepts.

The larger background against which this theoretical framework is to be understood is a world in which a monumental quest for social purpose is going on, in which multiple cultural manipulations are taking place, and in which powerful forces are thrusting all human groups toward standardization. Concomitantly, however, the desire to assert cultural diversity is operating even where it has long lain dormant.

The following chapters trace a line linking a pioneer in development ethics to a modern sociologist who has redefined the morality of subversion and on to a discussion of the new ideology adopted by religious thinkers and institutions in many Third World settings.

Notes

1. See Denis Goulet, *Etica del Desarrollo* (Montevideo: IEPAL, 1965); idem, "Ethical Issues in Development," *Review of Social Economy* 24, No. 2 (September 1968): 97-117; idem, *The Cruel Choice, a New Concept in the Theory of Development* (New York: Atheneum Publishers, 1971).

2. David E. Apter, *The Politics of Modernization* (Chicago: University of Chicago Press, 1967), p. 6.

3. George W. Wilson, ed., *Classics of Economic Theory* (Bloomington: Indiana University Press, 1964), Introduction, p. 12.

4. Marquis W. Childs and Douglass Cater, *Ethics in a Business Society* (New York: Mentor Books, 1963), p. 33.

5. From *Patrologie Grecque*, ed. by Migne, Tome XIX, Homily 12 on Paul's First Epistle to Timothy. Cited in L. J. Lebret, *La Montée Humaine* (Paris: Les Editions Ouvrières, 1958), p. 183, n. 9.

6. See Robert L. Heilbroner, *The Worldly Philosophers* (New York: Simon & Schuster, 1966), pp. 10-11.

7. Ernest Becker, *The Structure of Evil* (New York: George Braziller, 1968), p. 34.

8. Wilson, *Classics of Economic Theory*, p. 23. He adds: "The need to curb the acquisitive instinct is obviously less important in an expanding economy, and it slowly became perceived that the achievement of expansion might require a dismantling of feudalistic and mercantilistic restraints—or at least a drastic change in their form. The road to *laissez-faire was a long and devious one, but when economic growth in general and a higher degree of economic security became established facts the entire attitude toward the national economy changed. It was then possible to reduce restraints against individual profit-seeking. Economic thought thus became less ethical and more analytical.* (Emphasis mine.)

9. This is not to ignore, of course, the role of the Puritan ethic in encouraging entrepreneurship. The statement refers to formal economic doctrine, which prided itself on analyzing inner workings of economic systems.

10. Heilbroner, *Worldly Philosophers*, p. 130. On p. 142 Heilbroner adds that "shorn of its overtones of inevitable doom, the Marxist analysis cannot be disregarded. It remains the

gravest, most penetrating examination the capitalist system has ever undergone. It is not an examination conducted along moral lines with head-wagging and tongue-clucking over the iniquities of the profit motive—this is the stuff of the Marxist revolutionary but not of the Marxist economist. For all its passion, it is a dispassionate appraisal and it is for this reason that its somber findings must be soberly considered."

11. Adolf A. Berle, Jr., *The 20th Century Capitalist Revolution* (New York: Harcourt, Brace and Company, 1954), p. 166.

12. John Kenneth Galbraith, *Economic Development in Perspective* (Cambridge: Harvard University Press, 1962), p. 43.

13. See James K. Feibleman, *The Institutions of Society* (London: George Allen & Unwin, 1956), p. 61.

14. Ernest Gellner, "Reflections on Philosophy, Especially in America," *Worldview* 16, No. 6 (June 1973): 49.

15. The major works of Adam Schaff, Leczek Kolakowski, Roger Garaudy, Ernst Bloch, Ernst Fisher, *et al.* clearly reflect conventional Marxist attitudes in the technology debate. See, for example, A. Zvorikine, "The Laws of Technological Development," *The Technological Order*, ed. Carl F. Stover (Detroit: Wayne State University Press, 1963), pp. 59-74. For a more nuanced position, see Radovan Richta, *Civilization at the Crossroads: Social and Human Implications of the Scientific and Technological Revolution* (Prague, 1969).

16. One should not be absolute, however, about Sartre's acceptance in underdeveloped countries. He has, after all, written the preface to Fanon's *The Wretched of the Earth* (New York: Grove, 1963). See also, A.A. Fatouros, "Sartre on Colonialism," *World Politics* 17, no. 4 (July 1965): 703-720.

17. Alvaro Vieira Pinto, *Consciência e Realidade Nacional* (Rio de Janeiro: Instituto Superior de Estudos Brasileiros, 1960) 1: 65-66.

18. There are exceptions, of course, but the "exciting" Marxist social philosophers are precisely those who profoundly question orthodox Marxist ethics.

19. Etienne Gilson, *The Unity of Philosophical Experience* (New York: Charles Scribner's Sons, 1937), p. 306.

20. Thomas Kuhn, *The Structure of Scientific Revolutions*, (Chicago: The University of Chicago Press, 2nd ed., 1970).

Chapter II

L. J. LEBRET:
PIONEER OF
DEVELOPMENT ETHICS

L.J. Lebret was a remarkable man. I cannot undertake here a review of either his entire life or the
vast number of published works and institutional
creations he left in his wake. Fortunately for us,
these have been well documented by others.[1]

Lebret's Life and Accomplishments

A brief biographical sketch will do here. Louis-
Joseph Lebret was born in 1897 to a family of fishermen; his birthplace was the hamlet of Minihic-
sur-Rance near Saint-Malo, a major port of Brittany. Throughout his life he never ceased to display the qualities one associates with seafarers:
hardy respect for nature, boundless curiosity in
lands and cultures other than his own, unshakable
common sense in the face of life's tragedies, and
ever-fresh willingness to take new risks.

Lebret joined the French navy at eighteen; a

year later he entered the Naval Academy. During
World War I he saw active service off the coast
of Belgium and Holland and in the Middle East.
Afterward, he was briefly director of the port of
Beirut. In 1922 he was named an instructor at the
Naval Academy, where he rapidly gained a reputation as a gifted mathematician. The following year,
however, Lebret, now twenty-six, abandoned his
promising naval career to enter the Dominicans.
After ordination, he was assigned to the convent
of Saint-Malo, where he was supposed to rest
because of poor health. But men of Lebret's stamp
can never rest. He plunged headlong into the social
struggles of Brittany's impoverished fishermen,
whom he loved so deeply because they were his
own people.

Very rapidly Lebret concluded that the misery
and exploitation which surrounded him were not
ephemeral or accidental evils. On the contrary,
they had deep-rooted, structural causes. The De-
pression itself was but a traumatic symptom of
the contradictions inherent in world capitalist
economy. During the next decade Lebret inves-
tigated links between unemployment and the
fishermen's starvation wages, between the chaotic
local organization of fishing enterprises and the
international effort of large firms to monopolize
choice fishing banks, between the tremendous vul-
nerability of small fish merchants and the broad
market structures they could not control. By 1939
Lebret had personally conducted over four
hundred surveys of social and economic conditions
in numerous fishing ports, from the Baltic through
Great Britain to the Mediterranean. All the while
he was actively engaged, in tandem with a remark-

able fisherman-turned-political-militant, Ernest
Lemort, in creating a network of fishermen's labor
unions, maritime associations, cooperatives, and
groups working to restructure Europe's entire
fishing economy.

During this period he began to devise the unique
research methodology which was later to become
one of his hallmarks.[2] Conventional research tools
had proved of little help when his set task was
simultaneously to understand interlocking structures and to educate fishermen to assert mastery
over them. Furthermore, the vast local differences
he encountered between Denmark and Italy,
Tunisia and England, forced him to adopt proce-
dures of great flexibility which could readily be
adapted to various localities. Ever both a
philosopher and a mathematician, Lebret strove
to ally empirical measures with critical reflection
on the human values encountered in the real world
of people's everyday lives.

This vast labor was interrupted by the outbreak
of World War II. The French government drafted
Lebret to protect French fisheries and, later, to
help oversee its merchant marine policy. Shortly
after the German Armistice, Lebret, now living
in the unoccupied southern zone of France, wrote
The Mystique of a New World, in which he defined
his position *vis-à-vis* capitalism, nazism, and communism. The Vichy government censored the book,
allowing it to appear only in truncated form. After
the war it was published complete as *The Discovery
of the Common Good*.

During World War II, one of Lebret's major creations took form. In 1941 he launched, from Marseille, an interdisciplinary research center, Eco-

nomy and Humanism. Its scope included all the problems affecting a human economy—institutions and systems, the myriad forms of social change, ideologies, competing pedagogies, economic sectors, the dynamisms whereby a populace may play a role in decisions affecting its own conditions. Lebret was not alone in the endeavor; he was joined by economist Francois Perroux, peasant philosopher Gustave Thibon, agronomist J.M. Gatheron, industrialist Alexandre Dubois, and theologians Fabien Moos and Henri Desroches. The composition of the team was not fortuitous. As François Malley reports, Lebret sought:

> fruitful collaboration among professional theologians, economists and social scientists.... He had felt the need to call upon those who were competent, philosophically and theologically, to engage in a kind of in-depth reflection which required them to take some distance; it also required a level of technical and theoretical interests which could not be shared by team members more deeply committed to direct action.[3]

That during the German Occupation Lebret should have succeeded in recruiting such a remarkable team was a tribute to his talent for attracting powerful personalities and leaving them free to grow in their own direction. Lebret himself wrote:

> Coordination is doubly difficult at Economy and Humanism because we are a group whose fundamental principle is respect for the liberty of each one, for the vocation of each member. To take each person into account means to allow each one to achieve personal fulfillment in order to succeed in the total work.

Each one, therefore, will push ahead, take the initiative.[4]

This charism was later to win Lebret a multitude of disciples—even among many who had never worked with him directly—in Africa, Latin America, the Middle East, and Asia. After his death they sent testimonials, telegrams, and letters by the hundreds.[5] I myself can vouch that mere association with Lebret constituted intellectual and human stimulation of the highest order.

But let me return to Economy and Humanism in 1941. It was, perhaps, the first serious team effort at studying the multiple dimensions of what later came to be called the development problem. Its goal was to examine critically the theoretical and political bases of competing economic systems, to create instruments for linking the analysis of small units with an understanding of national or world units, to discover how social change could be planned in cooperation with a populace and in harmony with its values and objectives, and to discover guidelines for intelligent action at all levels. Such an ambitious enterprise, hampered by scarce resources, inevitably met setbacks. And, over time, respect for the personal vocation of each member of Economy and Humanism led to several partings of the ways; in 1945, Perroux, Gatheron, and Thibon moved to other tasks. Additionally, after the war the team made several geographical moves, dictated by the adjustments imposed by reconstruction throughout France. No one was more aware than Lebret himself of the difficulty in allying research to action, in keeping a team of secular and religious social scientists collaborating, especially when many resources—building, libraries, and personnel—were provided by the Dominicans. In his 1945 annual report, he summarized the group's polarities: internal cohesion and adventurous response to outside needs; administrative efficiency and the mystique of a movement aimed at transforming broad social structures; the requirements of scientific research and of popularization for the masses; a movement which was to open new possibilities for large numbers of people everywhere and a tightly knit party; members of the team who belonged to religious orders and those who were lay persons with families to support; volunteers and salaried personnel; the board of directors and the core staff; and finally, colleagues recruited from working or peasant classes and others whose style and approach were more bourgeois.[6]

We may grasp the breadth of the enterprise by examining the manifesto published by the founders of Economy and Humanism in 1942. After denouncing the structural bankruptcy of liberalism and state socialism alike, the authors declare:

> We believe that dead-ends exist only in systems, not in the facts. The problem has been erroneously formulated both by neo-liberalism and by neo-socialism. Authority and a *distributive* economy do not necessarily mean a *statist* economy at the national level. Nor do *market* and *free economy* necessarily mean an *omnipresent* market and the *tyranny* of price. To define a communitarian [form of] economy is, therefore, to liquidate these errors and to set in their place a positive construction. Terminological dishonesty and verbal confusions are so prevalent that we deem it necessary to define our own vocabulary and to distinguish terms which are often treated as equivalents: *corporatism*, the *corporation*, *community*.[7]

The document then analyzes in detail what the authors understand by community, by an economy based on need and service to humans rather than on growth or profit, by the status of property in such an economy, by the organizational units needed to maintain human scale in exchanges and production, and by the research tasks facing the group if it is to base its projections in the real world of complex technology and rapid communications. We can discern here the imprint Lebret left on all his creations—the powerful synthesis of thought and action, the sweeping vision allied to a patient regard for detail, and the critical analysis of structures joined to a perceptive understanding of the range of human motivations in diverse cultural settings.

The 1942 manifesto of Economy and Humanism is not without shortcomings. In retrospect, one finds its conceptual framework too closely tied to the closed economy which characterized a wartime, occupied, two-zone France. Besides, some of the basic themes—the rejection of a profit economy, the need to transform social structures radically, the vital distinction among diverse kinds of needs—are still framed in terms derived from the period's dominant ideologies. Nonetheless, as Wladimir d'Ormesson wrote in *Le Figaro*, the document brought a fresh wind of hope to a humiliated France.[8]

Today, thirty years later, Economy and Humanism is still a vigorous institution. Through its bimonthly review, books, and public training sessions, it continues to disseminate research findings to a wide constituency. After the lean early years it now enjoys a solid reputation as an interdisciplinary research, teaching, and action center. Its research emphases are the European economies, the sociology of change, new pedagogical methods, and the training of personnel for mobilizing social change.

By the 1950s, however, Lebret's own attention had begun to focus almost exclusively on the problems of the Third World. This interest led him to new activities and new creations.

Lebret first experienced what he called "the shock of underdevelopment"—traumatic, existential contact with mass misery—in 1947, during his first trip to Brazil (where he had been invited to give a course on the "human economy.") He asserted that, compared to the poverty one found in Brazil or India, even the poorest of the poor in France were privileged beings. And if he had judged the economic structures of Brittany in 1929 oppressive and dehumanizing, how was he to assess these structures in their most brutally destructive manifestations in Asia, Latin America, or Africa? They were manifestly incompatible with that "common good" and that "human economy" which were the central themes of his research.

Lebret had never doubted that a system based on the quest for profits was incapable of satisfying human needs. And he had an instinctive ability to grasp the ramifications of local problems. He could see unemployment in a fishing district or low productivity on a backward farm and learn anew the workings of international monetary structures or patterns of world managerial recruitment. Conversely, he never rested content with macroeconomic analysis or sectoral studies; these, he insisted, must be translated into terms which

could be related to family budgets and the living
conditions of concrete men and women, into the
effects policies and programs have on emotional,
cultural, and spiritual values. One Argentine
sociologist accurately portrays Lebret as one who
"preferred to produce facts over believing in postures, who understood the world through a permanent praxis and who taught that the most Christian and the most genuine form of humanism is
to struggle to satisfy the needs of humankind."[9]

From that first trip to Brazil until his death in
1966, Lebret undertook countless missions as a
development advisor to Brazil, Colombia, Vietnam,
Senegal, the Malagasy Republic, Lebanon, Vene-
zuela, Chile, Uruguay. Wherever he went, he
trained local teams to carry on the task of critical
research allied to transforming action. But in his
view something more systematic and permanent
was needed. Accordingly, in 1958, he founded
IRFED, the Institute for Research and Training in
Development. Working closely with Economy and
Humanism, IRFED was intended to prepare future
leaders of the Third World for the difficult tasks
of development. They would study, serve field
apprenticeships, and return home to undertake or
resume their developmental responsibilities. Their
central concern was always to be the causes of
and the cures for underdevelopment. Today's
IRFED has evolved considerably, especially since
Lebret's death. It has bifurcated into two separate
organizations.[10] One, still called IRFED, centers its
efforts on development education, regional development studies, and experiments in linking
grassroots efforts with national or sectoral

development plans. The other offshoot is called Faith and Development; it examines the role of religion and religious institutions in the processes of social change throughout the world.

During its early years, IRFED bore the personal stamp of its founder. It approached development education on the following premises:

• All individuals preparing themselves for committed development work need to be acquainted with the assumptions and methodology of all the major disciplines—economics, planning, human geography, cross-cultural sociology, politics, nutrition, demography, and so on.

• Even analytical and theoretical studies should be oriented toward the transformation of social reality.

• The value implications of competing development models, strategies, and programs need to be criticized explicitly in the light of prevailing ideologies and political doctrines.

• No true interdiscipline can be achieved by a mere juxtaposition of partial viewpoints.

Accordingly, IRFED sought an organic unity of diverse disciplines, joining reflection to action and microanalysis to macroanalysis. Students engaged in practical field work around a specific problem—irrigation, industrial planning, new curricula, medical treatment, or the like. The underlying aim was to produce a form of scholarship which was responsive to urgent human needs. Only thus, Lebret thought, could developers be prepared to undertake humanizing forms of change. Developers were to be tough-minded yet tender-hearted, professionally competent yet compassionate, and experienced in grassroots reality.

Identical premises underlie Lebret's major writings on development, *Concrete Dynamics of Development, Suicide or Survival of the West, Development-Revolution in Solidarity* and his voluminous reports on development in Colombia, Lebanon, Vietnam, Senegal, and Brazil.

Some of his best-known books, however, have another character: they are works addressed specifically to Christians committed to the task of building social justice in history. Their very titles evoke their special tone and content: *Action, Movement Toward God; The Human Ascent; Dimensions of Charity; Rejuvenating the Examination of Conscience; Civilization; The Summons of the Lord; Guidebook for Militants.* In these books Lebret reveals himself to be a powerful mover of men or, to paraphrase Kierkegaard, the "town-crier of prophetic vocations." Indeed, he was never embarrassed to speak of prophecy, of commitment, even of love. But it had to be "intelligent love," for, he said, intelligence without love can only breed a brutalizing technocracy which crushes men, whereas love without disciplined intelligence is inefficient, leading to amateurism, well-intentioned bungling, and, ultimately, catastrophe. The reason is that chronic structural evils cannot be corrected by subjective good will, but only by a concerted transformation of structures, a task which presupposes a rigorous and detailed understanding of how structures work. Lebret refused to accept the simplistic choice: *either* efficiency *or* humanization. He understood that efficiency was indispensable; but he also knew that it had to be redefined so as to serve human values.

After Lebret's death, on July 20, 1966, one French writer compared him with Teilhard de Chardin.[11] The differences between the two men are patent: Teilhard was a loner, whereas Lebret was a gregarious leader of team efforts; Teilhard had disciples, Lebret had partners who continued his work. But both were pioneers in essentially secular areas of study, to which, however, each brought a cosmic vision anchored to his religious view of human destiny. Each had to do battle against the conservative mainstream of the religious institution to which he belonged. Each set for himself rigorous scholarly standards which challenged the conventional wisdom of peers insensitive to history's larger movements. And, to a considerable degree, each was a prophet unhonored in his native land. (Lebret's influence in Latin America, Africa, and Asia far outstrips the relatively mild interest in him shown in France.)

Among the international development establishment, Lebret was usually treated as an interesting marginal figure, although he was, at times, invited to address important United Nations conferences and other world development assemblies. Notwithstanding such minor tributes as the posthumous publication of an article in *International Development Review*,[12] he was never granted the full professional recognition which was his due as the creator of dynamic new theoretical and practical approaches to development. One reason was, of course, his refusal to observe the prevailing canons of scientific "objectivity." More important, he was too prescient. It took the development community decades to rally to his basic insights, to the considerations that Lebret had placed at the heart of his diagnosis and prescriptions more than forty years ago:

● Development is, above all, a task of forging new values and new civilizations in settings where most existing institutions contradict human aspirations.
● The only valid path is to seek optimum growth in terms of a population's values and in terms of resource limitations.
● Planning is futile unless it is a permanent association between decision makers at the summit and communities at the grassroots.
● Equity in the distribution of wealth and the achievement of dignity for all are priority targets of development efforts.
● Conflicts of interest can be solved only by eliminating privilege and launching a general pedagogy of austerity.

The Salient Themes

In the pages which follow, I will elaborate on these major themes of Lebret's and evaluate, however summarily, his contributions to the study and practice of development. Underdevelopment, in Lebret's view, is not mainly an economic problem; neither is it simply the inability of social structures to meet the new demands of formerly passive populations. Above all else, underdevelopment is a symptom of a worldwide crisis in human values. Development's task, therefore, is to create new civilizations in a world of apparently chronic inequality and disequilibrium. Lebret calls such creation the "human ascent," meaning ascent in all spheres of life—economic, political, cultural, personal, and spiritual. It requires new patterns of solidarity which respect differences and do not posit any easy shortcuts to the elimination of privilege and domination. Monumental human intervention must occur, aimed at optimizing the use of all resources—natural, financial, technical, and human—if a human economy is to be implanted in small localities as well as in more extensive regions, in national societies as well as in the world at large.

The Crisis in Values and a Scale of Human Needs

"The problem of the distribution of goods," Lebret wrote in 1959, "is secondary compared to the problems of preparing men to receive them."[13] Underdevelopment bears witness to the bankruptcy of the world's economic, social, political, and educational systems. Not only have these systems created mass misery coexisting with alienating abundance; they have also reified human beings and subordinated them to the myths of growth and social control. Therefore, although rational planning, judicious investment, new institutions, and the mobilization of the populace are necessary to achieve development, such measures can never be sufficient. More necessary is overall cultural revolution in the values human beings hold. To Lebret it was evident that underdevelopment is a byproduct of the distorted achievements of those societies which incorrectly label themselves developed. He argued that satisfying an abundance of false needs at the expense of keeping multitudes in misery can never be authentic development. Rather, a sound hierarchy of needs must be established for every community. These needs must harmonize with the community's spiritual and cultural values, with the exigencies of solidarity with others, with the demands of wise resource use, with the aspiration of all individuals and groups to be treated by others as beings of worth independent of their utility to those others.[14]

Lebret distinguished three categories of needs:

- Essential subsistence needs (food, clothing, housing, health care, and the like).
- Needs related to comfort and the facilities which render life easier (transportation, leisure, labor saving-devices, pleasant surroundings, and so on).
- Needs related to human fulfillment or transcendence, whose satisfaction confers heightened value on human lives (cultural improvement, deeper spiritual life, enriching friendships, loving relationships, rewarding social intercourse, and so on.) These may also be called "enhancement goods"; they enhance human societies qualitatively and find their expression in cultural or spiritual achievement.

The policy implications which flow from this vision are obvious:

- Basic development efforts must place priority on assuring all persons sufficient goods of the first category. This priority ought to dictate investment decisions, the kinds of social systems adopted, the mechanisms of world resource exchange, and the allotment of scarce resources to competing groups.
- Sufficiency at the first level must not be pursued

to the detriment of goods related to human fulfillment. Lebret insists, however, that the satisfaction of basic subsistence needs is the prerequisite
or infrastructure upon which human creativity
and expression normally depend if they are to
flourish.

• The second category of goods, ranging from goods
which are relatively useful to those which are lux-
uriously wasteful, is not totally useless but should
be clearly subordinated to the others.

This attention to priority needs is precisely what
is absent in the major competing economic systems. Capitalism, even refined or corrected, is
responsive through markets to two forces: the
effective purchasing power of those who already
have more than enough, and the ability of pro-
ducers to manipulate the desires of potential consumers. There is no mechanism for collective decisions or for critical analysis of desires to determine
if they meet genuine needs or alienate human
satisfactions.

Centralized socialism also fails, but for different
reasons. By and large, it has subscribed to the
mass-consumer myth in its efforts to catch up with
the United States. Moreover, it has downgraded
the importance of noneconomic values and those
values which do not collectivize existence, to the
detriment of spiritual, artistic, and personal
growth. This deficiency is nowadays amply acknowledged by Marxist heretics, such as Alexander I. Solzhenitsyn, Leszek Kolakowski, Ernst
Bloch, Roger Garaudy, Adam Schaff, and others.

The few efforts at decentralized socialism of
which we have knowledge have not advanced very

far, although the Chinese have attempted, in their Cultural Revolution, to educate people to free themselves from the allurements of technological efficiency and the enticements of material affluence. More specifically, Mao Tse-tung has tried to persuade his people that austerity is a permanent component of any authentic socialist humanism.[15] But the pressures in the opposite direction remain strong: most people are incapable of tolerating austerity except as a necessary evil in the early stages of capital accumulation. And once affluence is desired—even for the distant future—it may well become impossible to mobilize development efforts on the basis of moral incentives and solidarity with one's needier fellows. There is grandeur, no doubt, in Mao's vision, but it may be too optimistic because it is based on such a heroic form of asceticism. Even the Christian religious orders vowed to poverty in the hope of eternal gain have not resisted the lure of goods.[16]

Lebret understood that levels of human need are not static but dynamic and progressive. Yet men and women must first grow in order to have the absorptive capacity to "have more" without "becoming less" human. This value perspective on development necessarily led Lebret to contest the validity of the development achieved in mass-consumer societies. Not only does such development beget underdevelopment, but even "what appears to be, in terms of human values, anti-development."[17] Consequently, any development strategy or policy must radically revolutionize the goals and processes by which needs are defined and satisfied. Otherwise, it can at best produce only palliatives; at worst it will create new patterns of mass alienation and dehumanization.

Here, in my opinion, is the central axiom in Lebret's ethics of development: all human beings in every society are entitled to enjoy the structural and institutional conditions which foster universal human ascent.[18] He never tired of quoting with approval the phrase coined by Francois Perroux —"development is for all men and for the whole man."

The Human Ascent and the
Creation of New Civilizations

Human progress, to Lebret, is no historical necessity; it is always achieved by human wills struggling to master the determinisms they face from nature, from their own limitations, from the social systems they have forged, and from their own technological and cultural artifacts. In other words, progress or "development" takes place when growing freedoms can find their expression in institutions, norms of exchange, patterns of social organization, educational efforts, relations of production, and political choices which enhance the human potential. What is ultimately sought are the basic conditions under which all persons may fulfill themselves as individuals and as members of multiple communities.

Notwithstanding his evident sympathy with Marx's view of the nonalienated society, Lebret rejected what he took to be a truncated model of humanism which considered spiritual and personal excellences only in their bastardized expressions.[19] Like Teilhard de Chardin, he believed that to imprison human destiny within the confines of an immanentist view of history is to close the door to genuine transcendence; in effect, it diminishes the stature of man. Viewed in the light of modern Marxist humanists, such as Ernst Bloch, Ernst Fischer, and Leszek Kolakowski, it is clear that Lebret's position is fully compatible with that of vanguard neo-Marxists. Lebret saw freedom as simultaneously an end and a means: an end because men are not fully human unless they make themselves free; a means because they can use their freedoms either to fulfill or to demean themselves, either to build community or to oppress others, either to transcend themselves and make history or to function as mere consumers of civilization.

As a profoundly religious man, Lebret firmly placed hope in the liberating potential of authentic religion. One of his favorite themes was *dépassement*—the ability of each human being to overtake or transcend his own limitations and reach a higher level of achievement, perhaps even reaching the level of mysticism. There is a vibrant Promethean quality to his portrait of the fully developed person and developed society, as there is to the profiles sketched by Marx, the revolutionary humanist, and by Teilhard, the cosmic poet of evolution. Because of his hope in transcendence, Lebret never accepted the mass-consumer model of development or any form of socialism which unilaterally stressed an egalitarian society primarily in terms of partners in production To him, opening toward metahistorical transcendence was a requisite of the full blooming of development potentialities. There was nothing sectarian or doctrinaire about this approach: he was not preaching some twentieth-century version of the Christian commonwealth. On the contrary, he appealed to persons of every ideological and religious persuasion—including those who gloried in calling themselves nonideological pragmatists or secular humanists. He called on everyone to grasp the historical grandeur of human destiny as an adventure in possibility. He believed it possible for men to eliminate misery, to create just structures, to devise educational systems which free men to "be more," to create exchange mechanisms which foster reciprocity, to prepare a new breed of developer whose loyalty is to the masses and who is tough-minded (as he must be if the technical complexities are to be mastered) while remaining tender-hearted (as he must if compassion and human communion are to influence decisions which necessarily involve high costs in human suffering). Developers of this calibre could serve at all levels as ferments and catalysts of new action, as educators of themselves and of others in an ascending spiral of human growth in responsibility, moral grandeur, and emotional, rational, and esthetic expression. The ideal, Lebret conceded, might never be reached, but the direction was unmistakable. The creative energies released in the effort societies make to reach that ideal are what creates history. What a mistake it would be, therefore, to consider development simply as modernization or as an effort to overcome an economic or technical lag. No, development is the historical quest for new values, new institutions, and a new culture in each society; it elicits new norms for interaction within and among societies; its mandate is nothing less than to prepare a new universe and a whole galaxy of new civilizations.

In Lebret's thought, the nexus between development and the creation of new civilizations is so intimate that he could only define the former in terms of the latter. He further asserted that his definition is anchored in essential human values, and, consequently, that it is valid for all social groupings, from village to nation, and for all cultures. In a variety of works, he repeatedly defined development, with but slight variations, as

> the series of transitions, for a given population and all the sub-population units which comprise it, from a less human to a more human phase, at the speediest rhythm possible, at the lowest possible cost, taking into account all the bonds of solidarity which exist (or ought to exist) amongst these populations and sub-populations.[20]

Under this definition, the discipline of development becomes the study of how to achieve a more human economy.[21] The expressions "more human" and "less human" must be understood in the light of a distinction Lebret considered vital: the difference between *plus avoir* ("to have more") and *plus être* ("to be more"). In translation one cannot do justice to this terminology, but its message is unmistakable. Societies are more human or more developed, not when men and women "have more," but when they are enabled "to be more." The main criterion of value is not production or possessions but the totality of qualitative human enrichment. Doubtless growth and quantitative increases are needed, but not any kind of increase or at any price.

The world as a whole will remain underdeveloped or will fall prey to an illusory antidevelopment so long as a few nations or privileged groups remain alienated in an abundance of luxury (facility) goods at the expense of the many who are thereby deprived of their essential (subsistence) goods. When such situations prevail, both rich and poor suffer from insufficient satisfaction of their "enhancement" needs.

One grasps the scope of Lebret's concept of development by reflecting on the attributes he regards as essential to it. If it is to be genuine, he asserted, development must be:

● *Finalized.* It must serve the basic finalities, namely, to build a human economy, to satisfy all human needs in an equitable order of urgency and importance.

● *Coherent.* All major problem sectors must be attacked in a coordinated fashion. There can be no sacrifice of agriculture to industry, of one segment of the population to another. (This does not rule out a strategy of deliberately unbalanced growth, provided it is judiciously pursued and constantly rectified.)

● *Homogeneous.* Even when revolutionary innovations are introduced, they must respect the people's past history and their present capacities. No elitist imposition from above, in total rupture with a people's cultural heritage and absorptive capacity, is justified.

● *Self-propelling.* Unless development leads a society to the capacity to direct itself autonomously, it is invalid. This demands a battle against dependency, parasitism, passivity, and inertia.

● *Indivisible.* There is no development unless all the people benefit from it, unless the common good is achieved. Privilege systems, excessive gaps between the city and the countryside, alienating divisions of labor are all ruled out.

The policy implications of these attributes are, of course, as far-reaching as Lebret's very concept of development.[22]

Conclusion

This portrait of Louis-Joseph Lebret as the pioneer of development ethics does not, I fear, do him justice. I have said nothing of his imaginative approach to development planning, nor have I explained what he meant by optimum resource use: the harnessing of idle resources, the elimination of waste, the mobilization of latent energies, the establishment of new development poles, the integration of regions and zones into a network of "dynamically structured space." I have also failed to describe his contributions to the ethics of technical assistance, his theory of education for development, his methodological innovations in microanalysis (the portrayal of the situation in health, nutrition, transport, services, cultural life, and income by graphic circular diagrams eminently suited to public education). Furthermore, I have been silent about his model for multispecialty teams—some mobile, some permanent —operating at various geographic levels (local, small region, great region, entire nation, multinational units). My despair grows because I have not even hinted at his reflections on the proper role to be played by the United Nations and other world organizations, and by voluntary agencies such as churches, labor unions, student groups. I am also frustrated by my failure to present—even in summary—the many other development themes which Lebret touched upon, not only with grace but with insight, realism, and creativity. Among these are the role of single-party government in Africa, the proper modes of development aid and technology transfers, the criteria for selecting leaders within ministries. The list goes on and on.

My difficulty can be traced to the fact that Lebret stands as a giant in an infant discipline. Not that he had no defects or that his work was perfect. How could this be, since he was but human? One major failing was his inability to imagine that others, even intimate colleagues, could not perceive as clearly as he the panoramic synthesis between the small issue and the big problem, or the synthesis of the links tying everything together. Another defect was the excessive complexity and heaviness of his methodological instruments, a weakness he openly acknowledged.[23] And to those who did not know him or realize his many personalities, his works at times sounded technocratic, at times politically naive. Indeed there was something naive about him: it was the naiveté of one who never gives up on human beings no matter how deeply they have interiorized myths of their own making. But his political instincts constantly grew more sophisticated and critical, especially after his missions to Vietnam (1959–61) and to Lebanon (1960). As for the charge of technicism, it is simply mistaken. As I have written elsewhere:

One of Louis-Joseph Lebret's supreme glories is to have been simultaneously a wise man, a planner and a technician. His greatest glory, however, is to have been a man—fully a man—and a friend to all "groups," all peoples, all civilization. Solidarity and universality—these are what he lived.[24]

By 1966, Lebret knew he was fatally ill. He yearned only to live two more years, long enough to complete four books he had planned.[25] He never finished them. I regret, in particular, that his projected synthesis on the ethics of development was never written. As one who has labored to trace a path through the thickets of development ethics, I know that Lebret's book would have made a difference. Whenever he did something, whenever he met someone, it made a difference. This is the measure of a man.

Notes

1. See François Malley, *Le Père Lebret, l'Economie au Service des Hommes* (Paris: Les Editions du Cerf, 1968); P. Viau, ed., *1897–1966—Le Père Lebret* mimeo (Paris, 1966); Thomas Suavet, *Actualité de L.J. Lebret* (Paris: Les Editions Ouvrières, 1968).

2. One of his most influential books, now out of print, is *Guide Pratique de l'Enquête Sociale*, 3 vol. (Paris: Les Editions Ouvrières, 1950–55).

3. Malley, *Le Père Lebret*, p. 68.

4. *Ibid.*, p. 67.

5. For a representative sampling of these, see Viau, *Le Père Lebret*.

6. See Malley, *Le Père Lebret*, pp. 72–77.

7. L.J. Lebret, Rene Moreux, et al., *Manifeste d'Economie et Humanisme* (Marseille, 1942), p. 15. Translation mine.

8. See Malley, *Le Père Lebret*, p. 58.

9. Floreal H. Forni, "La Transcendencia de la Obra de L.J. Lebret," *Comunidad* 4, no. 32-34 (June-August 1966): 100.

10. For more information on this split, see *Développement et Civilisations*, no. 47-48 (March–June 1972), pp. 179-183.

11. See René Laurentin, "Non moins important que Teilhard," *Le Figaro* (Paris), November 15, 1966.

12. L.J. Lebret, "Développement et Civilisations," *International Development Review*, December 1966, pp. 22-24.

13. L.J. Lebret, *Manifeste pour une Civilisation Solidaire* (Calurie: Editions Economie et Humanisme, 1959), p. 49.

14. Lebret expounded his theory of scaled needs in many works, notably in "Pour une Economie de Besoins," *Economie et Humanisme*, no. 84 (March–April 1954); and *Dynamique Concrète du Développement* (Paris: Les Editions Ouvrières, 1961), pp. 121 ff.

15. See Roger Garaudy, *Le Problème Chinois* (Paris: Editions Seghers, 1967), pp. 224-27.

16. See Denis A. Goulet, "Voluntary Austerity: The Necessary Art," *Christian Century* 83, no. 23 (June 9, 1966): 748-52.

17. L.J. Lebret, "Editorial," *Développement et Civilisations*, no. 1 (March 1960), p. 3.

18. This is the burden of Lebret's *La Montée Humaine* (Paris: Les Editions Ouvrières, 1959).

19. See Malley, *Le Père Lebret*, pp. 55, 71.

20. Lebret, "Editorial," p. 1.

21. See Lebret, *Dynamique Concrète du Développement*, p. 40.

22. *Ibid.*, pp. 75-83, presents a detailed explanation of these characteristics.

23. See Malley, *Le Père Lebret*, p. 83.

24. Denis Goulet, "Lebret's Thought and the U.S. Presence in the Third World," *D&C*, no. 30 (June 1967), p.53.

25. See Vincent Cosmao, "Preface," in L.J. Lebret, *Développement-Révolution Solidaire* (Paris: Les Editions Ouvrières, 1967), pp. 8–9.

Chapter III

ORLANDO FALS-BORDA:
SUBVERSION AS
MORAL CATEGORY

In a letter to a friend in the United States dated May 16, 1969, Orlando Fals-Borda, a leading Colombian sociologist, made the following statement:

> I have been trying to disattach myself from portions of the North American heritage which I had received, and with which I find myself increasingly at odds. For this reason, I cannot identify myself with any institution of the United States that would uphold or sustain the present economic and social policies pursued toward the nations of the Third World.[1]

One year later this scholar declined an invitation to join Buckminster Fuller, Norman Cousins, Lester Pearson, Pietro Nenni, Jan Tinbergen, and other intellectual notables in a consultation group on the future of the United Nations. He gave three reasons for declining this honor. First, the United Nations is engaged in merely palliative efforts to overcome underdevelopment. Second, the group invited was conspicuously elitist, leaving no room for ideological dissidents or militant Third World university students. As a third reason, he cited his urgent need to return to Colombia in order to contribute "as far as I can, to the liberating effort to make my country a better place for its people, and to its search for autonomy and dignity. For me this task is of the highest priority."[2]

It is worth examining more closely the North American heritage that this Latin American sociologist was trying to flee. Born in the port of Baranquilla in 1925, he pursued his secondary studies at an American school there. In 1947 he received his B.A. in Iowa; in 1952, his M.A. from the University of Minnesota; in 1955, his Ph.D. from the University of Florida. This is the classic profile of a mobile Latin American intellectual with a multicultural education and international horizons. But, unlike many of his peers, early in his career this man had anchored his research in native rural field experience. From 1949 (when he was twenty-four years old) to 1951, he lived in Saucio, a small Colombian village of only seventy-seven households. From this experience he drew the materials for his study, *Peasant Society in the Colombian Andes*.[3] Years later he plunged himself even more deeply into the struggle of Colombian peasants for a livelihood, for land, for dignity, and for a voice in their own history. This fidelity, not to his class or to his profession, but to the people of his land, was at first hesitant and tentative, later consolidated. In later years, it led him to insert himself into the rural zones of *la violencia.* Out of this new experience came the landmark book, *Subversion and Social Change in Colombia*.[4]

This author and sociologist is relevant to our reflections on development ethics and Third World liberation because he has redefined subversion as a moral category. It comes as no surprise, therefore, that Fals-Borda dedicated the above-mentioned book to his friend and fellow sociologist, Camilo Torres, whom he labels "a moral subversive, the kind that blazes new paths." For Fals-Borda "dedication of this book to him is not merely an act of friendship but one of just recognition to the understanding of the meaning of the times in which we live."[5]

Orlando Fals-Borda, a thoughtful and active Protestant layman, is both a dedicated scholar and a committed agent of social change. His life in recent years has been an arena wherein conflicting loyalties have battled. One must beware of overstatement, of course, and avoid Manichaean imagery. Nevertheless, one treads safe ground in stating that Fals-Borda's life has exemplified three crucial choices:

- To be a detached scholar or an active revolutionary intellectual.
- To be an institutionally successful professional or a marginalized outcast. (One thinks instinctively here of Byron's tragic figure, "self-exiled Harold.")
- To be a "maker of history" or a Christian witness to transcendence.

Like my discussion of Lebret, my discussion of Fals-Borda is not intended as a portrait of the man. Instead, I shall discuss issues of vital importance to the ethics of development around two themes:

Fals-Borda's model of critical social science; and his life as a stage for ethical dilemmas and political choices.

Fals-Borda as Radical Sociologist

One striking paradox in Fals-Borda's career is the combination of his impeccable scholarly credentials[6] and his increasingly vocal assault on the pseudo-objectivity, the elitism, the ethnocentrism, the biases, and the distortions wrought in the name of objective social science. Lest we be misled by Fals-Borda's critique, we do well to document at the outset the high regard he has always maintained for intellectual rigor, for actual evidence, and for impartial verification. This is precisely why Borda is an important critic: he is no mere iconoclast, disillusioned by the political failings of his first vocation. On the contrary, his aim is to restore sociological thinking to what is best in its origins and to theorize, as Brazilian educator Paulo Freire puts it, "in the praxis mode." A few quotations from Fals-Borda's early work testify to his regard for social science.

The "Objectivity" of Social Science

When he launched his first field study, in 1949, Fals-Borda already knew that most government programs were based on subjective impressions or partisan interests. Accordingly, he wrote,

> It is important to have a sound knowledge of the facts and problems of rural life in Colombia. This empirical knowledge is needed in order to arrive at so-called

"scientific" legislation, and in order to plan intelligent campaigns and formulate intelligent policies. Precise diagnosis is the logical and indispensable preliminary to any possible prognosis. Healthy results cannot be expected when neither the disease nor the medicines are well determined.[7]

In 1966 Fals-Borda lectured in New York on "The Ideological Biases of North Americans Studying Latin America." Although he denounced the mystification wrought by conventional sociology, he nonetheless insisted that he was no enemy of the scientific method. On the contrary, he pleaded for a committed social science which favored radical change:

What is needed in Latin America and other developing countries is a science committed to development, with its practitioners identified with the national struggles to build a new and better social order. There are illustrious forebears in this regard, whose example is stimulating. It was a committed sociology and a committed social science that enhanced the contributions of such men as Malthus, Smith, Comte, Marx, Ward, Ortega and even Durkheim (the last chapter in his book on suicide is entitled "Practical Implications"). We need to go back to Ward to borrow the term "teletic." This is the kind of research we need: teletic, anticipatory, or projective research. We need to study the actual performance of institutions against the mirror of future needs and unachieved goals. This is not a new approach. It is found in engineering and industrial psychology, where it is called "quickening" and "systems research."[8]

Once again, in his major work, *Subversion and Social Change in Colombia*, Fals-Borda argues:

there is no solution other than to examine the situation with new objectivity, derived from the application of the scientific method to problematic and conflicting expressions of reality . . . . Knowledge is coveted not as an end in intself but for the purpose of projecting for the future a better society than the one we have now.[9]

There is no mistaking the target of Fals-Borda's criticism. He does not denounce sociology because it is objective, but because it betrays its professed goal of objectivity and negates existing values in the reality it studies. He calls for a return to historically rooted scientific study. Because their work lacks such roots, most social scientists err when they brand extralegal agents of change as subversives or deviants. Such labeling has, he writes, "been formulated in such a way that it becomes an element in the justification of the prevailing social order of a given historical moment. He who subverts is anti-social, no matter what the condition of society or the justice of his challenge."[10]

Fals-Borda argues that social science should not avoid value-laden or conflictual questions. Such flight is tantamount to ignoring reality. Moreover, it buttresses the interests of the privileged in societies whose basic structures are inequitable. What is required instead, he says, "is a sociology and a history [which], far from being instruments of domination and traditional exploitation, serve the nation thanks to the serious and arduous application of scientific methods, so as to help it escape from economic and intellectual colonialism, a spiritual vacuum, and the cultural and technical prostration which frustrate it as a people."[11]

This leads him to conclude that "to eliminate from the idea of subversion its traditional immoral ingredient is to provide a scientifically productive concept."[12] The reason is that purpose is inherent in social phenomena. Conflict, moreover, is implicit in all strategic endeavors for collective self-improvement; consequently, only a model of social disequilibrium does justice to the social realities. Fals-Borda rests his hopes on new patterns of sociological study because he believes that domination by privileged elites is facilitated by the passive ignorance of the populace, an ignorance which can be broken down only by serious sociological investigation. Understandably, therefore, in societies like Colombia, dominant groups consider sociology to be a "subversive science."[13] At present Fals-Borda frankly advocates a form of action/research which is openly committed to revolutionary transformation of Colombia's social structures. In his view, to engage in "neutral" or "objective" social science is simply to mask one's loyalty to the prevailing imperialist system.[14] Accordingly, subversion, as newly defined, is the moving power behind a wide range of efforts at radical correction of social ills.

Fals-Borda is not alone in attacking the alleged objectivity of social science. One thinks of Gunnar Myrdal: he criticized his own value assumptions while writing *Asian Drama* and enlarged on these reflections in a later work, *Objectivity in Social Research*. Alvin Gouldner, in *The Coming Crisis of Western Sociology*, likewise points to the need for a consciously value-committed mode of research. And the radical caucuses which proliferate within the professional associations of United States social science further testify to scholars' disaffection with studies unrelated to present-day struggles.

"Research with the People"

Revitalized social science must incorporate the subjective perceptions of committed agents of change into its quest for objectivity. The precise manner of doing this still remains undiscovered.[15] But Fals-Borda's field experiments have begun to point the way. Of pivotal importance, in his view, is conducting "research with the people."

One conventional form of field research is participant observation, wherein the researcher observes social reality by sharing the life of the community under study. Although Fals-Borda has engaged in participant observation in the past, he wishes to push one step further and advocates full "insertion" in the milieu to be examined.

What precisely does "insertion" entail? At the very least, it means accepting the ordinary conditions of life endured by the populace being studied. In Saucio, Fals-Borda performed farm chores and dressed in the typical *ruana* (a kind of poncho), khaki pants and boots.[16] More important, he explains, "I made a point of never trying to appear excessively different or superior; by doing this, I was attempting to close the cultural gap which exists between the educated Colombian elite and the mass of *campesinos*, a gap which, needless to say, is one of the reasons for their mutual misunderstanding and antagonism." He even altered his mode of speech so as to eliminate traces of class superiority. He "harvested wheat and dug potatoes with the farmers, frequented the *tiendas* and played *tejo*, sang ditties and danced in local fiestas, attended Mass with the people, became involved with their quarrels and disputes with outsiders, accompanied them in their sorrows as well as in their joys." The only badge of full acceptance he never won is that of the godfather: he never became *compadre* to anyone, thus proving "that, in spite of my efforts, I did not become a complete insider."[17] But one is entitled to wonder whether the refusal of this honor was not due to the fact that Fals-Borda was a Protestant in a Catholic village.

Such "insertion," however, may still remain superficial. What is more significant is that the researcher fully identify with the goals and values of a group committed to change, especially radical change. This is the stance Fals-Borda has presently adopted and it is that of the independent research institution to which he is attached, ROSCA. (Even the choice of the name reveals his eagerness to be identified as an agent of change; in the colloquial language of Colombia, *rosca* is a clique, a somewhat maligned "in-group" thought to be "up to no good." ROSCA's researchers are overtly identifying with maligned and oppressed groups—Indians and peasants—or the ideologically active elements in labor unions.) Thus, when Fals-Borda argues that research must be conducted "with the people," he means in allegiance to the cause of the masses and against the interests of their exploiters. He pushes the principle to its

highest degree by "inserting" himself in the midst
of peasant groups actively engaged in the struggle
for land, justice, and power. For Fals-Borda and
his ROSCA colleagues, "insertion" ultimately
requires social scientists to become actors in the
process they study in accord with the political decisions they have taken. In their own words:

> Insertion conceived as a technique of observation
> and analysis of processes and factors includes,
> within its ambit, militancy aimed at achieving cer-
> tain social, political and economic objectives. It is
> currently being practiced by researchers whose in-
> tention is to bring about, with greater effectiveness
> and understanding, the changes which are neces-
> sary in society. Simultaneously, insertion as tech-
> nique incorporates researchers to popular groups,
> no longer in the old exploitative relationship of
> "subject and object," but rather in a mode which
> values the informational and interpretative input
> of the groups studied. These groups, moreover,
> have the right to use the data and the other ele-
> ments obtained in the course of the research.[18]

These declaractions notwithstanding, however,
one may question whether Fals-Borda carries the
principle of "research with the people" to its fullest
implications. It does appear that he still uses
research instruments primarily as dictated by his
discipline, in contrast to the pioneer efforts of
Robert Caillot, Georges Allo, and others whose
approach is designed specifically to allow the population studied to define the research agenda and
the hypotheses to be studied.[19] In their work, the
people's own perceptions take precedence over
those of the trained scholar in formulating
researchable questions. Nevertheless, Fals-Borda

and his ROSCA associates have recently worked
with new research instruments designed by the
very people being studied. Fals-Borda refers to the
people as being "self-studied."[20] Under this formula, Colombian peasants ferret out their long-
forgotten recollections of past events, reconstruct
the history of their earlier struggles against land
owners, and interview members of their own community with a view to confirming the tentative
interpretations of the trained researchers who
adhere to their struggle. Afterwards illustrated
pamphlets, profusely illustrated and using simple
daily language, are produced.[21]

When he speaks of "research with the people,"
Fals-Borda advocates political commitment to a
definable cause which is of benefit to the masses
who are exploited or oppressed. By so doing, he
castigates both rarefied, ivory-tower research and
any form of theorizing which is divorced from social
praxis. During the research process, however, he
does not relinquish the special claim of social scientists to the validity and legitimacy of their professional endeavors. Fals-Borda once told a ques-
tioner in the United States that, while studying
violence in rural zones controlled by revolutionary
guerrillas, he had had to struggle mightily to
defend the legitimacy and the merits of his scientific research on subversion. One interesting foot-
note to this tension is the experience of Fals-
Borda's friend, Camilo Torres, also a trained
sociologist. Even before he became an active
revolutionary combatant, Torres had written at
length on the distinction between his role as a
Christian and as a priest (to make normative value
judgments) and his task as a sociologist (to describe
reality as he finds it without meddling in value

judgments). And yet, the central point of that essay was to highlight the positive social effects of subversion and violence.[22]

Subversive Violence as a Positive, Institution-building Force

A third facet of Fals-Borda's vision of a critical sociology is the insistence with which he characterizes violence as a positive force for social change. Social change is immanent to societies in virtue of their very existence. Such change may take a variety of forms: it may be endogenous or exogenous, spontaneous or guided, evolutionary within a given system or designed to overthrow the status quo. "Change becomes subversive only when it is fostered by rebel groups committed to the transition from one social order to another."[23] Borrowing the language of religion, Fals-Borda calls subversion a modern form of heresy. To him, Jan Hus and Thomas Munzer are "symbols of subversion-as-heresy."[24] Their present-day successors are Fidel Castro, Mao, Guevara, Ho Chi-Minh, Marighela, Cabral, Torres, and countless others. Their models of subversion are, of course, profoundly moral, as evidenced in their writings and their lives of sacrifice so that others may enjoy justice. Hence the counterviolence they are obliged to employ does not destroy social welfare; rather, it removes obstacles to the construction of authentic social good. Lest we fall prey to the stereotypes prevalent in our own bourgeois culture, Fals-Borda warns:

The guardians of the established order often forget that many subversives have in time become the heroes of a new society and the saints of a revitalized Church. Their attitudes and beliefs had not been accepted in their own time because these threatened vested interests. With historical perspective, the anti-social elements are seen to be others: those who defend an unjust social order, believing it to be just only because it is traditional.[25]

Not only is subversion the forerunner of social construction; it is the vital moral force which transforms passivity and exploitation into human dignity and liberation. A supreme sense of moral worth pervades the subversive enterprise in Latin America. "Subversion represents a real possibility for renovation, freedom and collective fulfillment. It may afford a chance for Latin America to find itself and follow its own way in the univeral concourse."[26]

On the other hand, too many "legal" and "proper" measures for change are mere palliatives and self-defeating summons to failure. Consequently, there can be no doubt that subversive groups in Colombia constitute the "key category" of agents of change.[27]

What is most noteworthy here is not the argument Fals-Borda makes; the same case has often been made by others. But Fals-Borda articulates his case in the very terms of conventional sociological wisdom. He attempts to show, in myriad ways, that even in the eyes of social scientists subversives must not be viewed as "deviants," "aberrants," or "marginals," but rather as constructive agents of social change. Thus, Fals-Borda himself acts as a linguistic subversive within the arena of sociological discourse. And, like all subversives, he glories in the label!

The Pull of Conflicting Loyalties

Historical circumstances have conspired to make Fals-Borda's professional life an arena of conflict in which his loyalties are deeply divided. Born into a Presbyterian family in the most conservatively Catholic nation of Latin America, he was understandably attracted to the American schools with which Protestant missionaries are largely identified in Colombia. More important, he was born in an age of transition for Latin American social science: from a stage of infancy to immediate adulthood. As a young man with a bachelor's degree, he quickly learned that jobs were scarce for a sociologist with his skills. He describes the experience as follows:

After a very brief period of service with the United Nations pilot project at Viani, Colombia, in 1949, I approached other Colombian agencies that could use sociologists. Their number was, of course, quite limited, and it did not take very long to exhaust the possibilities of doing any kind of sociological work in connection with established institutions. Finally, I accepted a job as an assistant to the manager of the Sisgo Dam works, then under construction by Winston Brothers Company for the Caja de Credito Agrario, Industrial y Minero, a government agency.[28]

He explains that

Winston Brothers Company, constructors and engineers of Minneapolis, Minnesota, who have engaged in work in Colombia since 1925, and who have been an important asset in the material development of the country, made it possible for me to gather data

at Saucio and then to present the material at the
University of Minnesota.[29]

During the years that followed, his personal
growth was intimately tied to his mobility within
the ranks of sociology, United States style. Fortunately, his burning desire to be sociologically
objective and relevant led him to seek first-hand
knowledge of peasant realities in Colombia. This
was later to produce a painful cleavage between
his aspirations to scholarship and his commitment
to social justice. As a close personal friend and
professional colleague of Camilo Torres, Fals-
Borda was directly touched by that man's great
and tragic destiny. Torres' political and religious
choices constituted for Fals-Borda a direct summons to shoulder his own burden in history's present moment.

*The significance of Fals-Borda's drama lies in
this: it is not merely a personal one, but it typifies
the choices faced by a whole generation of Third
World scholars as they acquire a new critical consciousness of their society's problems.*

There can be no justification for trespassing into
the inner sanctum of a man's conscience in order
to understand the subjective factors which produce moral choices. Accordingly, I shall not violate
the privacy of a living man, still active in Colombia,
who is both an admired scholar and a respected
friend. But Fals-Borda himself has repeatedly
urged students of social change to confront head-
on the taboo subjects of ethical dilemmas, value
conflicts, and criteria for decisions which lie in the
shadows of sociological research. This is why I feel
no qualms about examining his *public* writings and
his *public* decisions, with a view to analyzing the

structure of ambiguity within which serious moral agents inevitably find themselves nowadays. And Fals-Borda's conflicting loyalties do provide an *objective* arena in which today's social forces exercise their conflicting pulls. Several such conflicts deserve comment here.

Scholar or Committed Agent of Change?

Fals-Borda's work and life contain lessons for others because he strives to remain *both* a scholar and a committed agent of change. I noted before the importance he attaches to an "objective examination of Colombia's rural problems." In his first book he voiced the complaint that "Colombian literature is rich with eloquent descriptions of the *campesino,* his way of life, his customs, his beliefs. But nearly all these descriptions have romanticized him so much, certainly with good intentions, that it becomes difficult sometimes to tell where fancy ends and reality begins."[30]

Twenty-three years after that Saucio study, he continues to base his scholarship on direct contact with peasant communities, now near Montería, in northeast Colombia. His fidelity to the demands of scholarship abides; he is never one to despise the merits of theory. Neither does he endorse the view which would confer legitimacy solely on active militancy. His intelligence is too fine and his critical spirit too richly endowed to accept, even in the name of revolutionary commitment, any simplistic anti-intellectualism.

One instinctively recalls here the division of labor in the Bolivian mountains when Che Guevara forbade Régis Debray, the fragile but sometimes over-zealous French bourgeois-intellectual-turned-revolutionary, to take up arms. He was more important in the revolution, said Che, as a writer and publicist. More striking still is the testimony given by a Colombian student who abandoned her university studies and joined the guerrilla army. In an unpublished letter to a friend, a Protestant monk in Taizé, she writes:

> Contemplatives, in the name of all mankind, in the name of the continents which struggle for their authentic liberation, in the name of revolutionary politicians, of world masses and students, in the name of scientists, of intellectuals, or artists, I ask this of you: Do not be afraid to live your vocation, do not be ashamed to continue to live it intensely, do not snuff out that light which you have uncovered and of which the world has need.[31]

Whatever the division of labor or one's specific forms of commitment, there is, as Brazilian educator Paulo Freire has often noted, no valid theory without praxis. Conversely, without theory, militancy can only be sterile activism. In Fals-Borda's unending struggle to reconcile scholarship with militant involvement one feels a pervasive and critical sensitivity to the dialectical complementarity between the word and the deed. This is the meaning of his militant research founded on dialectics.

> Commitment is in no way a matter of rebellion against classical scientific method because basic principles of inference are observed and the control of intervening factors and elements is sought. Objectivity is also

maintained, within adequate bounds.... The primary reason for a scientist to adopt this position of commitment to social change and identification with the processes of socioeconomic development of a country is to be found in the verification that these processes have a purpose or *telos* whose transcendence and meaning may be understood only through active participation in them.... However, there is a limitation to this method that should be mentioned in order to be able to equally anticipate its efforts.... The projections derived from the use of telic research in sociology may come to have the characteristics of a "prophecy" that conditions or engenders its own implementation. This phenomenon of self-fulfillment is not experienced outside the world of the superorganic and constitutes a real factor that may impinge upon forecasts made. To establish further, through inquiry and well-controlled special work, the divergencies between the actual prediction and its implementation, in addition to discovering what part is conditioned by the publication of the results, could be a task of great scientific interest in the sociological field.

In any case, the use of this method, even with the dangers of its self-determination, would reduce the total amount of oversight to manageable proportions and would open the possibility of leading collective action toward previously established goals in a conscious manner.[32]

Fals-Borda does not claim that revolutionary social change is best served by scholars, merely that *he* can best serve it by critical scholarship. Like other committed intellectuals, he asks in return only that those who are committed in other ways not reduce revolutionary authenticity to their own mode of struggle—a tendency often manifested, alas, by political militants. There is no only way to be a revolutionary!

Institutional Professional or Creative Outcast?

This second tension derives from the first. Surely it is important for any committed agent to decide for whom he or she is working, in whose interest, and at whose expense. For the most part, the question can be answered only by evaluating the political and ideological stance of the *institutions* within which one could operate. Nevertheless, one cannot be a purist or a fundamentalist in this regard; there are degrees of collaboration with institutions, just as there are limits to the alternatives one may find or create.

One central feature in Fals-Borda as a case study in conflicting loyalties is his conscious decision to remove himself from the institutions wherein he could normally have expected to exercise his talents very fruitfully. He has severed his ties with the National University of Colombia, has made the broad accusation that universities, at least in Colombia, have become "factories to produce personnel for capitalist imperialism."[33] His choice testifies to a conviction that his energies should not be placed at the service of palliatives for the ills of underdevelopment. At times, former colleagues in the academy or in international service have criticized him for this choice. Yet it is worth pointing to Fals-Borda's extraordinary tact, discretion, and restraint, even after he had severed himself from old connections. He never judges or condemns those who choose other options.

A few examples will illustrate this point. Fals-

Borda is a skilled and experienced professional: he helped found the modern Department of Sociology at the National University of Colombia· in 1959; he has served as a visiting professor or lecturer at Columbia University, at the University of Wisconsin, at the London School of Economics, in Chile, Cuba, and Sweden; he has acted as programme director at the United Nations Research Institute for Social Development. Hence the significance of his decision to become, in some sense, an institutional outcast. It is simply a risk he must run to be true to his commitment to radical social change in Colombia, Latin America, and the rest of the Third World. He did not take the step with a light heart, nor does he disdain communication with those who have remained within conventional scholarly circles. For he knows that these circles, too, must be revolutionized, from within as well as from without.

His seemingly moderate position regarding this conflict of loyalties has even led some of his fellow Colombians to criticize him, to claim that he was so compromised by the establishment in his earlier years that no one will fully trust him now, neither the left nor the right. As far as I am able to judge, however, this accusation is completely unjust. It overlooks two crucial realities. First, Fals-Borda is a man of deep moral sensitivities. As such, he understands the difference between subjective responsibility for his own choices and objective judgment about historical institutions. Second, as one who has witnessed violence at first hand, he is not tempted to glamorize or idealize it. More important, his sense of history prevents him from assuming a posture which at first glance might seem heroic or pure, but which over time would isolate him from those very masses whose consciousness must be transformed if revolution is to become possible. Therefore, he is not indifferent to results and to effectiveness. Accordingly, he is trying to work where results are possible and where the specificity of his own contribution can complement the labor of others. This is why he repudiates in the sharpest terms all improper or unfocused kinds of "insertion" in the populace. Many agents of change are nothing more than manipulators or agitators whose ultimate purposes and loyalties are incompatible with the genuine liberation of those they profess to help.[34]

To condemn Fals-Borda because his position seems ambiguous is to misunderstand the structurally ambivalent condition of any society in the travail of unprecedented social change. This sociologist is not sure he will become a complete outcast from professional institutions, but he is willing to run that risk. And above all, if he must be an outcast, he wants to be a creative one who contributes to the liberation of the oppressed groups.

Advocate of Violence or of Christian Reconciliation?

No arena of conflicting loyalties is more troubling, especially to Latin Americans, than that of revolutionary violence. On the one hand, serious advocates of social change recognize the permanent systemic violence perpetrated on the populace by repressive regimes serving a privileged social structure. Consequently, they readily accept the view that revolutionary violence is basically a form of counterviolence which is, at times, necessary to create the very possibility of justice. Moreover, they understand that the social impact of advocating nonviolence is to favor the status quo and deprive opponents ... of the established order of the legitimacy and the weapons with which they could wage their battles.

In this regard, Fals-Borda repeats Guevara's distinction between the moral system of the guerrilla and that of the regular army soldier. "Essentially," writes the Colombian,

> they differ in commitment: the former is willing to offer his life to the cause and forego all comforts, while the second is a simple mercenary. Moreover, the use of violence is conditioned to the resistance shown by the reactionaries who impede the birth of the new society; thus, the guerrilla is not a violent man *per se*, and should not be confused with a bandit. He uses counter-violence, that is, the revolutionary violence of the just rebellion, or the just war. Therefore, on moral grounds his superiority may appear undeniable ....
> It is under this light that painful acts like the kidnapping of foreign ambassadors and national personalities by truly revolutionary groups should be understood. Counter-violence of this type depends on the violence executed previously by reactionary groups in power .... The strategy of subversive war therefore requires to respond in kind to the onslaughts of those who oppose radical progress because this social change would end their selfish, vested interests. If there were less selfishness, in theory, there would be less violence. But resistance to change and the establishment of more repressive regimes in the area thus far anticipate even more violent encounters.[35]

Most of Fals-Borda's work, however, takes

revolutionary violence for granted, as simply a
necessary instrument for achieving subversion
and the new social order. Whatever his private
reflections on the matter may be, his writings do
not reflect the dramatic anguish of conscience one
detects in the writings of Camilo Torres. Fals-
Borda accepts subversion as a historical social process, endorses its objectives, praises its heroes, and
reinterprets it as socially constructive, without
bothering, in his own name, to justify violent
means in the name of ethics or religion, or even
good politics, as Torres does. In this sense, he is
very much more the historical analyst than Torres.
Fals-Borda, in fact, keeps his distance from the
practical arguments over violence, as evidenced
in the following passage:

> It is impossible to enter here into the polemic over
> the justification of the use of violence, which has been
> going on for several centuries . . . .Nor is it necessary
> to turn to the classical thesis of Saint Thomas
> Aquinas concerning the just war, even though it is
> important to recall the way in which it was revived
> in the sixteenth century to legitimate the Spanish
> conquest and the Christian subversion . . . . Trans-
> lated to present situations of internal conflict in
> which the control of the social order is fought over,
> the same positive argument for the use of subversive
> violence appears.[36]

Later in this passage, Fals-Borda evokes Lenin,
Kautsky, Ortega y Gasset, Marx, Torres, Hobbes,
and Max Weber. One definitely gets the impression
of a historian of ideas, not of a polemical advocate.
Nevertheless, both Fals-Borda and Torres state
categorically that the churches should line up on

the side of the oppressed. And for the two men, revolutionary violence is the violence of the just rebellion or the just war.

Yet on one vital point of interpretation, Camilo Torres and Orlando Fals-Borda disagree. This is on their assessment of the total impact of the years of *la violencia* in rural Colombia (1949–57). For Torres, *la violencia* was a major, positive force in transforming social structure and attitudes in rural Colombia. He concluded by saying that "violence has constituted, for Colombia, the most important socio-cultural change in peasant areas since the Conquest by the Spaniards."[37]

Fals-Borda, notwithstanding the central thrust of his sociological labors—that subversion is both a moral and a socially constructive category —seems to assess *la violencia* quite differently. He writes:

> In the end, *la violencia* was no more than a blind, leaderless conflict that undermined ancient customs of the peasant population, demolishing at the same time their yearnings for significant change and disorienting their angry reaction. It is improbable that this phenomenon was anticipated by the dominant groups, even with all the cunning at their disposal. But it undoubtedly served to alienate the people from the goal of their previous ideals. Even though there were efforts to channel and rationalize peasant violence and formally organize it, it escaped all bounds to the point of becoming a confused expression of predominately [*sic*] personal conflicts by peasants incapable of gauging the great transformation that might have been carried out. They could not seek the support of an ideology, and there was no national leader or any institution that might show them the way and redeem them from their deep tragedy.[38]

In other words, *la violencia* was not revolutionary violence and it did not serve the cause of subversion.

In my opinion, Fals-Borda's ethical values are no less historical and no less religious than Camilo Torres'. Like Ortega y Gasset, Fals-Borda can only bring himself to accept violence as "exasperated reason"; like Marx, he feels himself the "midwife of history." Torres preaches more overtly the utopian end of revolutionary violence: reconciliation in justice and brotherhood. Fals-Borda chooses to live in private ethical tension between the acceptance of violence and the call to limits. And when he discusses these issues, he treats them as historical *prises de positions* in the age-old debate. Marxist philosophy, which has been paramount in the evolution of his thought, offsets his early training in the sociology of Durkheim and Weber. Fals-Borda is thereby more easily led to the analysis of social conflict which, in his view, is the key to understanding the reality of underdeveloped societies.

Notes

1. Orlando Fals-Borda to James Lamb, May 16, 1969, Cambridge, Mass.

2. Orlando Fals-Borda to Norman Cousins et al., May 12, 1970.

3. Orlando Fals-Borda, *Peasant Society in the Colombian Andes* (Gainesville: University of Florida Press, 1955).

4. Orlando Fals-Borda, *Subversion and Social Change in Colombia* (New York: Columbia University Press, 1969).

5. *Ibid.*, p. xiii.

6. For Fals-Borda's impressive credentials, see the Colombian *Who's Who?: Quién en Colombia*, 3rd ed. (Bogotá: Oliverio and Cia., 1961), p. 189

7. Fals-Borda, *Peasant Society*, p. ix.

8. Orlando Fals-Borda, "The Ideological Biases of North Americans Studying Latin America", mimeo. (New York: University Christian Movement, 1966), p. 5.

9. Fals-Borda, *Subversion and Change*, pp. ix-x.

10. Orlando Fals-Borda, "Subversion and Development: the Case of Latin America" (Paper delivered as the 11th Annual Foyer John Knox Lecture, Geneva, 1970), p. 7.

11. Orlando Fals-Borda, "El por qué de la nueva edición revisada y puesta al día de *La Subversión en Colombia* (Bogotá: Ediciones Tercer Mundo), p. 7.

12. Fals-Borda, *Subversion and Change*, p. 9.

13. *Ibid.*, p. xi.

14. Orlando Fals-Borda, Victor D. Bonilla, Gonzalo Castillo, and Augusto Libreros, *Causa Popular, Ciencia Popular* (Bogotá: Publicaciones de la ROSCA, 1972), p. 13.

15. On this, see Denis Goulet, "An Ethical Model for the Study of Values," *Harvard Educational Review* 41, no. 2 (May 1971): 205–227.

16. Fals-Borda, *Peasant Society*, pp. 252–253.

17. *Ibid.*, p. 255.

18. Fals-Borda, Bonilla, Castillo, and Libreros, *Causa Popular*, p. 24.

19. See Goulet, "An Ethical Model."

20. Orlando Fals-Borda to the author, February 8, 1973.

21. Representative samples of such pamphlets are *Lomagrande, El Baluarte del Sinu*, 20 pp. (Monteria, Colombia:

ROSCA, 1972); *Tinajones, un Pueblo en Lucha por la Tierra,* 20 pp. (Tinajones, Colombia: ROSCA, 1973).

22. See Camilo Torres, "La violencia y los cambios sociocul- turales en las areas rurales colombianas, in *Camilo Torres,* Cuernavaca, Mexico, 1966, *Sondeos,* no. 5, pp. 10/112-177.

23. Fals-Borda, *Subversion and Change,* p. 21.

24. Fals-Borda, "Subversion and Development," p. 6.

25. *Ibid.,* p. 8.

26. *Ibid.,* p. 14.

27. Fals-Borda, "El por qué de la nueva edición," p. 5.

28. Fals-Borda, *Peasant Society,* p. 249.

29. *Ibid.*

30. Fals-Borda, *Peasant Society,* p. ix.

31. For obvious reasons this source cannot be made public.

32. Fals-Borda, *Subversion and Change,* pp. 203–207.

33. Fals-Borda, Bonilla, Castillo, and Libreros, *Causa Popular,* p. 34.

34. See *ibid.,* pp. 26–31.

35. Fals-Borda, "Subversion and Development," p. 13.

36. Fals-Borda, *Subversion and Change,* p. 166.

37. *Camilo Torres, Sondeos,* no. 5, p. 10/174.

38. Fals-Borda, *Subversion and Change,* p.144.

Chapter IV

CHURCHES, PROPHETS, AND THE THIRD WORLD

This chapter will attempt to outline the stances of present-day religious spokesmen and sketch the activities of certain Christian social prophets, political leaders, and development scholars, in an effort to identify the issues which have become crucial for Christian participants in the development debate.

The Churches Take a Stand

Until a decade ago, most influential churches and religious organizations aligned themselves with the status quo. This was true of the Catholic Church in Latin American, the Christian missions in Asia and Africa, and Christian denominations within the developed world. To describe precisely *how* Christian officialdom had come to this position lies beyond the scope of this essay.[1] But its posture was derived from the practice of adjusting to what

ecclesiastical theorists rather quaintly designate
as "temporal power." "Temporal power" means
simply the dominant political rulers. And in the
Third World, efforts at Christianization had relied,
by and large, on these very rulers for logistical
support. During the Spanish and Portuguese col-
onization of Latin America, the Cross had done
more than simply follow the Sword; it had ridden
the same ships and had received the same royal
subsidies. Less obtrusively, but no less intimately,
Christian missionaries from the West had pro-
selytized in the footsteps of imperialist colonizers
in India, Africa, and the Arab world. Rival Christian factions usually had won their entry into new
mission fields according to which colonial power
gained political or economic ascendancy. Thus
Catholics flourished in Indochina thanks to
France's control, whereas Protestants fared better
in India. Protestants gained a late foothold even
in Catholic Latin America in the wake of the new,
twentieth-century United States presence, con-
testing that of Spain, Portugal, and France.

The unholy alliance of churches with ruling
groups in Third World nations also correlates with
the degree to which religious institutions depend
on native upper and middle classes for their financial support. Usually these classes are precisely
those with the greatest vested interest in preserving extant social systems

Of equal significance is the general ideological
stance of the Vatican and of worldwide Protestant
bodies such as the World Council of Churches. Until
recently, it was almost anathema for their spokesmen to propose radical social reform, to challenge
existing social authority, to criticize economic

systems at their center rather than their periphery. Social enlightenment came to the World Council of Churches at roughly the same time as John XXIII launched *aggiornamento* in the Roman Church.

As long as conservatism had ruled at the summit, it was to be expected that grassroots churches should likewise prove chary of brutal ruptures with the ruling system. But a new era has set in: the encyclicals *Pacem in Terris* and *Populorum Progressio*, the Medellin Declarations, and the series of ecumenical meetings on development held in Beirut, Montreal, and elsewhere have created a new climate.[2] Nowadays it has become almost routine for churches to reject the conventional wisdom of the development establishment and to reconsider their own traditional posture towards the ruling classes. Most church spokesmen, it is true, remain conservative and "prudently" moderate in their positions on social change. The same is true of mainstream church membership almost everywhere. Nevertheless, dissident minorities are increasingly heard; they are thrusting their agendas even into the debates of the majority in church assemblies. Class struggle, ideological conflict, competing politics, diverse party alliances, and religious strategies at every level are now common experience in churches and religious organizations.

These recent trends are not the product, however, of intellectual breakthroughs by theologians. On the contrary, new theological and pastoral stances are the result of practical responses by specific Christian groups to the challenges posed by revolutionary movements, ideological militants, and guerrillas armed in struggle against repressive governments. Churches in the Third World have had no choice but to come to terms with the social forces shaping present history. Churches too must throw off the shackles of conservatism. As Dom Helder Camara, the archbishop of Recife, in northeast Brazil, explains in speaking of the populace:

> It is easy to retort that their eyes will be opened with us or without us or against us. If this happened tomorrow, and the masses of Latin America had the impression that Christianity was afraid, that it lacked the courage to speak out before the government and the propertied classes, they would reject Christianity because in their eyes it would clearly be an ally of their exploiters.

> The best way to combat Marxism is to teach a religion which is not the "the opium of the people"; to preach a Christianity which, in union with Christ and following his example, embodies and appropriates all human problems in order to accomplish man's redemption.[3]

Denounced by their own fellows who repudiate the ties of the church with governing elites and privileged classes, theologians, bishops, ministers, and lay people have been forced to redefine their stance towards temporal power, toward legitimate authority, toward the ethics of violence, toward the foundations of Christian hope, toward the meaning of history, toward the gospel itself.

Many readers are already familiar with the efforts of the major Christian denominations to resituate themselves as to what their mission is, especially their mission to those who are poor or

exploited. Events such as James Forman's manifesto to the United States churches are no longer
shocking news; neither does the creation of task
forces to evaluate the social and political effects
of church investment in South Africa surprise anyone. There is no need to discuss here what is common knowledge. Instead I shall comment on the
emergence into the public eye of three new types
of Christians: Christian prophets of development,
political leaders whose view of development is
directly linked to their Christianity, and scholars
whose Christian ethics inform their writings on
development.

Before doing so, however, I wish to summarize
the arenas wherein dissident Christians have
staked out new positions, contrasting with traditional postures. These new and vocal Christians
favor liberation over law and order, and they plead
for broad participation of the masses in taking decisions and actions for change, as opposed to elitist
or top-down models of planning. They reject
capitalism—even a capitalism which is rectified or
attenuated by welfare policies—as radically
immoral and structurally incompatible with social
justice. Therefore, they advocate socialism, however variously they define it. One of the values
they cherish most highly is autonomy—national,
regional, and local—in opposition to dependency
on outside forces. Moreover, they seek self-
determination which is not only political, but
economic, cultural, and psychological as well. Their
goal is to achieve egalitarian patterns of social
stratification, a program widely perceived by
hierarchical churches as subversive of internal
church order no less than of society at large. Theo-

logians of development and of liberation express their choices by critical new interpretations of history and by statements about Christians involving themselves in human tasks and constructing secular values in consort with groups that represent the wishes of the people—even when such groups are openly hostile to religion or materialistic in their philosophy. Such Christians are fond of John XXIII's distinction between "error and those who commit error, even if we are dealing with men whose ideas are false or whose inadequate notions bear [directly] on religion and morality."[4] (This reference is generally thought to apply to communists and is interpreted as permission from the Pope for Christians to cooperate with them in political and social matters.)

The commitment of militant Christians to liberation is not confined to rhetorical professions of principle or to new conceptual models for the conduct of theology. It finds its expression in everyday life: Dominican priests in Brazil offer sanctuary to urban guerrillas; Protestant missionaries in Uruguay actively support the Tupamaros; United States churches contribute funds to liberation groups in South Africa and Mozambique; priests issue public ultimatums to their religious superiors urging them to return church-owned lands to Bolivian peasants or to reject government subsidies for their schools. Such activists openly accept all political risks: suppression, jail, torture, exile, even assassination. They aim to prove to the world—and especially to those who were engaged in social militancy before they were—that they are serious about liberation, about "the combat for development."[5] In Chile, as in Tanzania, Yugoslavia, and

Algeria, Christian churches are being summoned by some of their own best members to help build socialism. If this new breed of Christians is labeled subversive for their troubles they have learned to glory in the label. Dom Helder Camara simply chuckles when Pope Paul VI greets him as "my communist archbishop." And Antonio Fragoso, bishop of Crateus in northeast Brazil, does not hesitate to write:

> If those who fight for justice are called subversive, then subversion is their hope. Tomorrow they are going to struggle for justice. Will they be on the side of subversion? The game is being played wrong. The flag of freedom, the flag of justice at this moment is being handed over into strange hands.[6]

The pattern is the same everywhere. Third World priests are denounced as communists by main-stream Christians in Argentina. Emilio Castro is viewed with ill-disguised suspicion by his more cautious Protestant peers in Uruguay. Maryknoll missioners Thomas and Arthur Melville and Blaise Bonpane are expelled from Guatemala. Daniel Berrigan is imprisoned by the state and ostracized by many of his fellow Jesuits. A mildly reformist bishop in Spain or Portugal is deported or stripped of his office.

The historical stage has been set for the reappearance of Christian social prophets.

Prophets of Development

Three years ago a course was instituted at Indiana University on Hebrew Prophets and Black

Messiahs. Black American church figures—Albert
Cleage, James Boggs, Ron Karenga, and others
—were placed in tandem with the Old Testament
prophets—Jeremiah, Amos, Ezekiel, Hosea. The
common thread of prophecy is the charismatic, personal vocation to denounce social injustice, punc-
ture the complacency of the powerful, defend the
interests of the weak and afflicted, and summon
coreligionists to return to the true God, to true
morality, to true righteousness.

Christians committed to social change increasingly appeal to ancient prophetic exemplars.
Protestant theologian Arend van Leeuwen has
argued that religion's major task today is to foster
what he calls *Prophecy in a Technocratic Era*.[7] But
theologians, preachers, and religious educators
also look to the New Testament to find the more
saliently prophetic passages. Latin American
theologians of liberation are fond of such texts as:

> The spirit of the Lord has been given to me, for he
> has anointed me. He has sent me to bring the good
> news to the poor, to proclaim liberty to captives and
> to the blind new sight, to set the downtrodden free,
> to proclaim the Lord's year of favor (Luke 4:18).

> My brothers, you were called, as you know, to liberty
> (Galatians 5:13).

Yet not all prophets are only preachers; on the
contrary, David, Hoseah, Jeremiah, and others
prophesied as eloquently by their deeds as by their
words. David ate the loaves of proposition, Hoseah
suffered an adulterous wife to mirror in his personal life Israel's infidelity to its God, and Jeremiah
shattered a clay pot in the sight of the nation's

leaders to symbolize that God would shatter their nation. Similarly, some modern development prophets are as well known for their actions as for their writings. This is true of Danilo Dolci, Camilo Torres, Sergio Mendez Arceo, Dom Helder Camara, and others. But I ought to make a qualifying statement here to avoid confusion. Not all modern prophets are social activists: some are contemplative monks, struggling to redefine the basis for their committed life of prayer, austerity, manual work, and solitude in terms of the structural racism, injustice and exploitation prevalent in the very world they have fled. One thinks here of Thomas Merton in his final years, of René Voillaume, of Daniel Berrigan, of dozens of monks and contemplative nuns in Taizé or in DeFoucauld fraternities throughout the Third World. Even cloistered monasteries have not been immune to the assault of the development debate.

With space enough, we could paint the portraits of a host of modern prophetic figures. Although the exercise would surely be instructive, a rapid overview may better convey the central truth, namely, that these figures are not anomalies or rare exceptions unrepresentative of a people at large. Far from being rare accidents, prophets, like theologians, are not makers of their age, but children thereof. They have achieved prominence because of the lived experience of throbbing human communities which lie behind them. It is true that prophets have always been the voice of those who have no voice, but they are heard only when the silent ones acknowledge those vicarious voices as their own.

Danilo Dolci, often called a Gandhi figure, is the

prophet of militant resistance to that special inertia bred of centuries of poverty and intimidation.
He is no church-going man, but, by his own declaration, has found nourishment for his almost mystical commitment to the poor in the gospels. In them
he has discovered a form of religion which brooks
no alienation—none of the passive superstition
which makes drought-ravished Sicilian peasants
rely on novenas instead of on irrigation pumps.
And Dolci will have nothing to do with God-figures
who serve as mystifying legitimizers of a religiosity whose social expression is paralyzing fear of
autocratic masters, be they semi-feudal landown-
ers or *mafiosi*. Although he is himself a powerful
father-figure, Dolci approaches social change via
an unlimited faith in the capacity of little people
to overcome fear and resignation, to evaluate their
own problems critically, and to organize pressure
on the powers above. On all these counts, Dolci
exemplifies major themes of the ethics of development now burgeoning in the praxis of revolutionary Christian communities. His testimony has dou-
ble value precisely because it is not "churchy Christian," in fact, it even has tinges of anticlericalism.
But it is not secular or irreligious: Dolci respects
the profound religiosity of his people and urges
them to create a purified, historically liberating,
new expression of it. His whole life is prophecy.[8]

Another interesting prophet of development,
likewise imbued with a deep Christian hope, is
Brazilian educator Paulo Freire. He is an eminently fit subject for a full length Christian biography. I mention him because he is the prophet
of *conscientizacão*, a radically critical conscience
and consciousness of the incarnate Christ of his-

tory. Freire labors incessantly to de-alienate "transcendence." His central vision of all human beings as "subjects, and not objects" of history subverts any pallid exegesis of Christian redemption. His hope in the ability of exploited, domesticated, annihilated victims of the "culture of silence" to free themselves is the political reflection of his acceptance of a divine Christ who truly makes man divine. Freire, more than any other social critic, any other political activist, gives forceful modern expression to St. Paul's assertion that "God has chosen the poor of this world to confound the rich, the foolish to bring down the wise." Freire serves as the living prophet of this Christian belief by his pedagogy of the oppressed, his strategy for liberation, his politics of historical transformation which is based on the oppressed themselves, on their ability to assume mastery over their own destiny even when they accept allies from the ranks of the oppressors. The latter defect from their class interests and provide documents, information, access to people, funds, and logistic support to those who must eventually free themselves. The totality of Freire's liberating cultural action bears witness to his belief (thoroughly Christian in its dialectical relationship to freely proferred divine grace) in the radical freedom of the human will, even when it has been enslaved for centuries.[9]

Few Christian prophets of development are so dramatic in their appeal as Camilo Torres: scion of a respected, bourgeois Colombian family, youthful playboy-turned-priest (parish priest at that, over the objections of his status-minded mother, who preferred the Dominicans), disciplined sociologist, university professor and campus minister,

reformist organizer and politician, and, finally,
guerrilla fighter. Torres' justification for joining
the liberation army goes to the heart of the question which concerns us here. In a declaration to
the press on June 25, 1965, following his request
to the cardinal-archbishop of Bogotá for permission to return to the lay state, Camilo Torres
argued that his priestly love of the people, especially the poor, had led him to revolutionary
struggle. "This activity is, in my judgment, essential for my life as a Christian and as a priest, and
as a Colombian."[10]

Camilo Torres chose the Christ of the oppressed,
the violence of the gospel ("I have come to set son
against father, brother against brother...."), the
Church of the poor. Reviled in life, revered in
death—Torres went the way of most militant
revolutionaries. But his dramatic decisions have
introduced a new variable into the ethical debate
on violence: no longer is it possible for Christian
moralists to condemn violence out of hand. So com-
pellingly did Torres embrace violence out of a specifically Christian commitment to justice and love
of the poor that anything less than existential
arguments appear very flimsy indeed. Torres sac-
rificed much when he resigned his priestly func-
tions, but, as he put it, how could he celebrate the
eucharistic memorial, the communion, until he had
first fought to make communion among men possible?

I am sacrificing one of the rights which I love most
deeply, that of celebrating the external rite of the

Church as a priest, in order to create the conditions which [would] render this cult more authentic.[11]

Was not any other form of worship hypocritical? Shades of Old Testament times, when the prophet could say: "Not incense or burnt offerings, but justice and pity are pleasing in the sight of the Lord."

Camilo Torres is a Latin American Christian honored by Fidel Castro, who has dedicated a school in Cuba named after the Colombian priest. Torres has had imitators among his fellow-priests—Domingo Lain in Colombia, and a few in other lands whose names remain secret. But his influence reaches far beyond his imitators: a whole generation of Latin American priests now measures the seriousness of its commitment to social justice against Torres as paradigm.[12]

I mentioned Dom Helder Camara earlier; he, too, is a typical Christian prophet of development in the Latin American mode. There is no need to summarize his achievements or repeat his message here, for Camara has become a world symbol.[13] He is the fragile David who slings outrages at a new Goliath, the Brazilian military regime; he is the voice of the silent ones in his own land, the conscience-pricker of Christians in the rich world, the galvanizer of dormant energies in the Third World. For many years Camara dreamed of mounting a massive nonviolent campaign of resistance against the structural violence of misery, unemployment, and illiteracy throughout Latin America. He argued that the reactionary ruling classes in Latin America, backed up by the military, diplomatic, and economic might of the United States, would easily crush any violent revolutionary movement once it was perceived as threatening by the stewards of the status quo. Hence he concluded that organizing nonviolent resistance was not only fidelity to the gospel, but hardheaded, realistic tactics. His dream never became reality because Martin Luther King was killed before he could accept Camara's invitation to visit Recife. Worse still, even the relatively mild protest actions organized by Camara in his own land have been stifled. His name may not be spoken in the Brazilian press except to defame him or to report some trivial, "churchy" news of no consequence.

Although silenced at home, Camara's voice has boomed out elsewhere in the Third World. And in Europe and the United States he has been a prophetic gadfly, calling upon students and development professionals to revolutionize their own structures if they would truly "help" the Third World, reminding them that the struggle for justice in society comes before brilliant professional careers. Above all, Camara has refuted the argument of those who would twist his nonviolent creed into a condemnation—however tacit—of the path chosen by Camilo Torres. As Camara himself wrote:

> I respect those who feel obliged in conscience to opt for violence—not the all too easy violence of armchair guerrilleros—but those who have proved their sincerity by the sacrifice of their life. In my opinion, the memory of Camilo Torres and of Che Guevara merits as much respect as that of Martin Luther King. I accuse the real authors of violence: all those who, whether on the right or the left, weaken justice and

prevent peace. My personal vocation is that of a pilgrim of peace, following the example of Paul VI; personally, I would prefer a thousand times to be killed than to kill.[14]

I must stop here, since I despair of being exhaustive. But a rollcall of Christian prophets of development would include other names: Camilo Moncada and Gustavo Gutierrez, Emilio Castro, Gonzalo Arroyo, and Rubem Alves. And I should have to add countless others in Africa, which I have ignored solely because my attention has long been riveted, almost hypnotically, on the turbulent Latin American continent.

Cynical and skeptical development professionals might contend that the religious prophets I have mentioned are marginal, at best, or that their influence on development struggles is minor. I believe this is mistaken. And the cynics cannot so easily dismiss the impact of two other categories of Christians who are deeply engaged in forging a vitally new and practical ethics of development. I refer to politicians and development scholars.

Politicians

Once again, the theme of this chapter—relating the ethics of development to Christian biography—tempts me to attempt too much—to try to do justice to the special contributions made to development thinking and practice by Julius Nyerere, Leopold Senghor, Tom Mboya, Eduardo Frei, Jacques Chonchol, and many others. We would learn much, I am sure, by comparing such politicians with the old-time political leaders whose Christianity was purely ornamental or instrumental. Politicians of the old school did not take Christianity seriously; they merely put it to political use, as did Bonaparte, Mussolini, and Franco. What is striking about the newer leaders is the degree to which each one's personal Christianity colors his notion of the exercise of political power and of the content to be given to his development program.

I am not implying that Nyerere and Senghor have chosen identical models; they certainly have not, although both aspire to create an indigenous African socialism. More striking still is the difference between Frei and Chonchol, whom we shall discuss shortly. These politicians all, however, have in common the fact that each man thought it necessary to determine what his politics ought to be in terms of his Christian beliefs. Their cases are so revealing precisely because they are so honest. Most politicians, in the recesses of their instincts, adhere to a theology of sorts, but they overlay this theology with verbal trappings and effective value commitments to Machiavellianism, Hobbesianism, Leninism, pragmatism, or "whateverism."

For this reason, it is worth a moment's pause to reflect on the development ethics of these new politicans. For illustrative purposes, I will confine myself to Nyerere and Chonchol.

Julius Nyerere's central themes are well known: self-reliance in education; the appeal to African tribal values as the moving power of development energies; the decision to accept slower economic growth so as to associate the whole populace with whatever growth is achieved; the stubborn refusal

to submit to the leverage, however subtle, of aid
givers, even at the cost of losing grants and loans;
the resolve to dynamize the countryside rather
than allow urban concentration to command
economic decisions and preempt professional services. These are not negligible themes. Neither are
Tanzania's policy choices to be viewed as insignifi-
cant in the larger puzzle of development
strategies. But here I prefer to call attention to
other contributions Nyerere has made to the
development debate. These contributions can be
traced, in my opinion, to his loyal attachment to
fundamental (though not fundamentalist) Christian ethical postulates.

The first trait in Nyerere's political style which
commands our attention is his truly remarkable
sense of detachment from preexisting development
models. The Tanzanian president seems equally
immune to the blandishments of capitalism and
the seductions of communism. Hence his unswerv-
ing insistence on the need to create one's own
model. It is as though he understood that, just
as religious conversion can only come from inside
a person, a nation's choice of a development path
must be self-generated. There is no questioning
Nyerere's commitment to socialism: it is clear and
irrevocable. But socialism is not what others
decree or export; it is what Tanzanians must build
themselves if they are to be genuine socialists, that
is, the architects of societal justice for all within
structures of freedom from alienation. As Nyerere
once wrote:

The Arusha Declaration is only a beginning. Tanzania is not now a socialist country; it is only a country

whose people have firmly committed themselves to building socialism. The actual work has barely begun. For socialism is not built by Government decisions, nor by Acts of Parliament; a country does not become socialist by nationalizations or grand designs on paper. It is more difficult than that to build socialism, and it takes much longer.[15]

Nyerere explains that socialism for Tanzanians is *ujamaa*, a Swahili word signifying "family-hood." The policies of other countries may be referred to as *kisoshalisti*—socialist. But, adds Nyerere,

By the use of the word "ujamaa," therefore, we state that for us socialism involves building on the foundation of our past, and building also to our own design. We are not importing a foreign ideology into Tanzania and trying to smother our distinct social patterns with it. We have deliberately decided to grow, as a society, *out of our own roots, but in a particular direction* and towards a particular kind of objective. We are doing this by emphasizing certain characteristics of our traditional organization, and extending them so that they can embrace the possibilities of modern technology and enable us to meet the challenge of life in the twentieth century world.[16]

Just as Nyerere views Christianity as embodying certain *universal* human values, notwithstanding its historical development in a particular cultural matrix, so, too, he argues that socialism is a *universally* valid term which captures the human aspiration for justice, dignity, and brotherhood.

Were we able to analyze in detail Nyerere's concept of austerity, his position on the relative merits of violence, and his belief about the need for secularism in a modern state, we would find, I suspect, deeply Christian roots. His stubborn insistence on human dignity as primordial is a repudiation of any ideology or political philosophy which would absolutize either politics or society itself. His stress on austerity—which he views not as a necessary evil in the early phases of capital accumulation but as a permanent component of authentic development—has deep Christian roots. Mao, it is true, made the same argument during the Cultural Revolution. But if we are to believe missionaries who knew Nyerere as a young man, he had reflected long and hard on the liberating message of gospel poverty. In short, Julius Nyerere presents a striking example of a Christian whose political stance is to a remarkable extent an expression of his ethics of development. He is no less critically attentive to the special forms of alienation found in socialism than to those which are more visibly attendant upon capitalism. Although he accepts the need for a strong state and a high degree of central power, Nyerere never idolatrizes or absolutizes that power. States must serve the people, and power must create justice. As he reflects on the monumental and nonrecoverable costs which often accompany social violence, Nyerere steers between the Scylla of complicity with structured violence under the banner of law and order, and the Charybdis of uncritical glorification of violence used to achieve revolutionary purposes. The Long March (this is the term he uses) of Tanzania must be an economic one. Although its people are deeply religious, the national task, and, therefore, the national state, must be secular. Otherwise it would be provincial, intolerant, and out of tune with the real forces of history.

Nyerere is simultaneously a very wise man and
a shrewd politician. Christians can derive at least
a small measure of satisfaction in learning that
the two qualities can coexist within the same person. They need to believe this, of course, even in
the face of most conventional secular wisdom
which denies the very possibility.

Jacques Chonchol is another interesting political
figure to study. An experienced agronomist/
economist, he appears to have three vocations:
skilled technician in his field (which is of vital
importance to development); practicing politician;
and Christian social philosopher. There is no evidence to suggest that radical changes have
occurred in the agronomist/economist side of his
personality, although his duties in recent years
have surely enriched his store of professional
knowledge. I am particularly intrigued, however,
by the main lines of his evolution as a Christian
social philosopher and a practicing politician. This
interest is dictated by the knowledge that the
Chonchol of fifteen years ago has evolved into a
public person who has put flesh and programmatic
concreteness on the new ethics of development and
the theology of liberation that we have been discussing so far. It is precisely because he has
changed so drastically—while not renouncing his
earlier principles—that Chonchol is a challenging
case study.

Chonchol has been active in Chilean politics for
nearly a decade. Shortly after Eduardo Frei was
elected to the presidency in 1964, he invited
Chonchol to return to Chile to help lay the theoretical and programmatic groundwork for land reform.
This seemed logical and natural since Chonchol

was a fellow Christian Democrat and an agronomist /economist with a combination of scholarly inclinations and zest for problem-solving field work. He had already made a reputation outside Chile; he had just spent several years working in Cuba under the auspices of the Food and Agriculture Organization and had written several books on development and land reform.[17]

During the first two years of Frei's presidency, Chonchol was a true believer in the merits of a third way of development, neither capitalism nor socialism. But the model failed: it lacked roots in real and contending social forces. Frei was sometimes bold in rhetoric, as was Kennedy in his early Alliance for Progress speeches, but he was timid in execution. His hesitations, however, were not traceable to personal defects or to a failure of nerve. No, the causes were structural. Frei had won his mandate because enough people who wanted far-reaching change had thought they could get it from him, and simultaneously enough conservative voters who feared "the worst" (socialism and Allende) thought it was safer to accept partial change under Frei, who was quite solidly committed to parliamentary democracy and free enterprise, than to risk losing everything should a more radical candidate win. Hence Frei's seemingly noble experiment failed because, despite the appearances, it was essentially a program of palliatives. Furthermore, he could not bring himself to overstep the ideological limits of his own Christian Democrat model of development.

Chonchol, on the other hand, quickly discovered that the third-way model could not work. He transcended his past ideological preferences and moved creatively, via a series of political quantum leaps, to a new position. Midway through the Frei regime, Chonchol left his position as director of research in land reform and withdrew from the Christian Democrat Party. Later he campaigned actively for Allende under the banner of MAPU, a small, new party with a commitment to Christian socialism. After Allende appointed Chonchol to the post of Minister of Agriculture, he left MAPU to help form the Christian Left Party, but this move does not seem to have had any major ideological significance. It has been explained by Choncol himself, and by his close friends in several parties, as a practical device to mobilize support for Allende in neglected floating portions of a potentially socialist electorate. What is decisively important in this political evolution, however, is Chonchol's repudiation of the third-way model and his unqualified acceptance of socialism as a valid form of humanism.

As a Christian social philosopher, he proved more dialectically attuned to history than Frei or than Roger Vekemans, Frei's leading intellectual mentor.[18] Less fearful of history's risks, willing to face whatever dangers may befall a Christian who cooperates with communists, Chonchol has turned full circle and his ideology is now fully integrated with that of the Chilean Christians for Socialism.[19]

Although he left the Ministry of Agriculture, Jacques Chonchol continued to be a practicing politician, a Christian social philosopher, and a development technician whose major interest is land reform. (The greatest feather in his politician's cap is the eighteen-month implementation of a radical land reform throughout Chile, on the strength of legislation that he had helped pass under Frei.) It is sometimes said that Frei made Allende possible. There is some truth in this: Frei's failures in 1964–70 doubtless made Allende's victory possible. But this is only half the story, since Allende's candidacy in 1964 also made Frei possible in that year. What is more germane to our present discussion of Christian ethics in the development debate is that the Chonchol of 1964–66 made the Chonchol of 1972 possible. There is hope here, living proof that Christian developmentalists need not be trapped in their own ideological heritage of reform. Without betrayal, but also without cowardice, they can move dialectically to positions which can realize the dreams of liberation theologians. Whatever may be Chonchol's future as a politician (and his position seems hopeless since Allende's death), his evolution in the past decade remains a paradigm of consequence.

Development Scholars

My treatment of the special contribution of Christian scholars to the development debate will be even more summary than my treatment of the prophets and the politicians of social change. This is partly because most Christian scholars, when writing about development, have *not* tended to be explicit about the Christian ethical framework they presuppose.

One may read, of course, such works as Gabriel Bowe's *The Third Horseman*, but the synthesis it attempts between economics and ethics is not very convincing.[20] Much writing on development by identifiable Christian writers is not rigorous and

falls easily into preachy moralizing. This is true
of religious conferences with development themes
and indeed of the papal encyclicals as well.[21]
Nevertheless, one ought to give the churches their
due. The educational materials they prepare for
their own constituencies have improved noticeably
in quality in recent years. And church writers on
such issues as foreign aid, world trade, and cor-
porate investment in the Third World sometimes
attain a level of impressive documentation and
sound scholarship. By and large, however, those
Christian writers on development whose professional credentials are unimpeachable have not
labored *ex professo* to *inform* (to breathe life and
form into) their work by a critical recasting of their
Christian ethics of development. Less systematically, nonetheless, several important professional
development scholars have brought profoundly
Christian categories into the development debate.

One patent example is Barbara Ward, the British
economist. A concern for social justice and for the
need to create conditions fostering human dignity
pervades her work. But it is when she emphasizes
the world community, the solidarity of all humans
riding spaceship earth, and the need for cooperation among all dwellers in the global village that
Barbara Ward evokes for us the mystical body of
the Christian religion—without, however, using
the term. One may reject Ward's consensus model
and her reluctance to accept conflict and discon-
tinuous social mutations as both necessary and
humanly good at times. But there is no gainsaying
her fervent universalism and her patient insistence on the need to forge new bonds of solidarity.
In addition to her writing, she has also worked

with several ecumenical Christian task forces on guidelines for church involvement in development, as have Jan Tinbergen, Robert Bowie, Robert Theobald, and a number of other development scholars.

Jan Tinbergen, the econometrician and planning theorist, is worthy of note. He was the first economist to receive the Nobel Prize. His work in economic planning mirrors the lifetime dedication of a man passionately committed to excellence and to the service of the entire human race. Tinbergen, a long-time socialist in his native Netherlands, attaches special importance to worldwide planning.[22] His concern is evidently consonant with the best universalist trends in Christian culture. At its best, this culture operates as a forceful corrective to ethnocentrism and narrow parochialism.

Other names also come to mind: French economists François Perroux, Destanne de Bernis, Jacques Austruy, Jean-Marie Albertini. Their writings contain flashes of the Christian social conscience and of the universalism I noted in Ward and Tinbergen. Equally important is these authors' acute sense of the inadequacy of purely economic or technical solutions to human social problems. Austruy, especially in *L'Islam face au développement economique*, draws attention to the manner in which *homo religiosus* behaves in response to economic stimuli.[23] Although Perroux repeatedly disavows speaking as a moralist and says he is only analyzing reality as it truly is in its existential complexity, he is in truth a development economist whose thought is informed by overtly Christian ethics. In development circles, his name is usually associated with the strategy

of "development poles," and his construct of
development as a dynamic three-fold process of
innovation/signification/propagation has proved
seminal for many students. But in such works as
Autarcie et expansion, L'Europe sans rivages, and
La coexistence pacifique Perroux conveys his faith
in a quasi-prophetic technological universalism
which no critical reader can divorce from Perroux's
tenacious Christian roots.

A growing number of scholars of Christianity
are making development their central topic of
study. One thinks of sociologist François Houtart,
of philosopher René Habachi, of theologians
Rubem Alves, Gustavo Gutierrez, Richard Shaull,
and, in recent years, Arend van Leeuwen. But
the crucial question for these scholars comes from
the development experts. Are their studies germane? Should development experts take their contribution seriously? Perhaps I can best answer by
narrating an episode. At an informal seminar I
attended several years ago, van Leeuwen kept
talking about development in rigorously theological terms. Several economists, political scientists,
and educational planners present expressed skepticism about van Leeuwen's credentials to speak
on the subject. But when he proceeded to tell of
his twenty-five-year experience as a missionary
in Indonesia, they were silenced by his overwhelm-
ing knowledge of grassroots economics and im-
pressed with his political acumen. An interesting
result was that one economist present, now director of Latin American studies at a large state university in the United States, drafted a paper on
the relevance of religious thought to development
economics.

That economist, at least, had clearly learned a

lesson; since then he has not ceased to inform his own reflections with sources he had previously chosen to ignore. Most development specialists, of course, remain indifferent to philosophical or theological studies on development and social change. This is lamentable, since both philosophy and theology are value-oriented and normative. Moreover, they are ambitious architectonic disciplines which place great value on synthesis. The values approach and the search for synthesis have been lacking in development studies, as Myrdal confesses so dramatically in *Asian Drama*. And it does appear that theologians, historians, and comparative religionists are beginning to make breakthroughs in development thinking.

This is why I hope that economists, political scientists, anthropologists, planners, geographers, agronomists, administrators, and financiers will soon begin to look more seriously to philosophy and theology for new concepts. And perhaps independent religious scholars, loosening themselves from their traditional moorings, will be freer than their peers in the social sciences to explore totally new perspectives and formulate illuminating interpretative schemes.

Conclusion

Christian ethics and Christian institutions have been challenged by the social forces which have thrust the Third World into the trajectory of history. Consequently, the development debate has become central to critical reflection on Christian ethics. The burning questions are numerous: Is social justice possible in a world of unequal wealth?

Should all persons share in decisions, or must development choices be left in the hands of a technocratic and managerial elite trained to achieve optimum efficiency and productivity? What moral standards ought to be used to decide how much and what kind of violence is necessary to achieve desired change? How does one measure a tolerable, as against an intolerable, human cost of development? What are the true dimensions of liberation and authentic development?

In the Third World today, one finds a seriousness and dramatic intensity in Christian ethical reflection which has heretofore been lacking. Interlocutors know that the stakes are high: the quest for human development has become increasingly coterminous with the struggle for liberation.

If the Christian reflective experience seems ambiguous, it is no more so than development itself, an ambiguous adventure *par excellence*. I, for one, do not know whether Christian ethics is contributing much to the development debate. But I am certain that the development debate is contributing greatly to the development of Christian ethics.

Notes

1. For an examination of this question, see such works as François Houtart and André Rousseau, *The Church and Revolution* (Maryknoll, N.Y.: Orbis Books, 1971); and Arend van Leeuwen, *Christianity in World History* (New York: Charles Scribner's Sons, 1964).

2. See, for example, "World Development, Challenge to the Churches" (Report of the Conference on World Cooperation for Development, Beirut, April 21-27, 1968).

3. Dom Helder Camara, *The Church and Colonialism* (Denville, N. J.: Dimension Books, 1969), p. 75.

4. Pope John XXIII, *Pacem in Terris* (Encyclical issued April 11, 1963), para. 158.

5. This is the title of a book written by a priest-economist, the late Laurent Turin, *Le Combat pour le Développement* (Paris: Les Editions Ouvrières, 1965).

6. Dom Antonio Batista Fragoso, "The Gospel and Social Justice," mimeo. (Address delivered in Belo Horizonte, January 22, 1968), p.9.

7. Arend van Leeuwen, *Prophecy in a Technocratic Era* (New York: Charles Scribner's Sons, 1968).

8. Among Dolci's many works, the following are especially useful in interpreting his approach to development: *Waste* (New York: Monthly Review Press, 1964); and *The Man Who Plays Alone* (New York: Pantheon Books, 1968).

9. See Paulo Freire, *Pedagogy of the Oppressed* (New York: Herder & Herder, 1970); *Cultural Action for Freedom* (Cambridge: Harvard Educational Review and Center for the Study of Development and Social Change,1970); and *Education for Critical Consciousness* (New York: The Seabury Press, Continuum Books, 1973).

10. Camilo Torres, *Camilo Torres*, Cuernavaca, Mexico, 1966, *Sondeos*, no. 5, p. 24/286.

11. *Ibid.*, p. 24/287.

12. For works in English about Torres, see German Guzman, *Camilo Torres* (New York: Sheed & Ward, 1969); and John Alvarez Garcia, ed., *Camilo Torres, His Life and His Message* (Springfield, Ill.: Templegate Publishers, 1968).

13. See José de Broucker, *Dom Helder Camara, The Violence of a Peacemaker* (Maryknoll, N. Y.: Orbis Books, 1970).

14. Camara, *The Church and Colonialism*, p. 109.

15. Julius K. Nyerere, *Freedom and Socialism, a Selection from Writings and Speeches 1965-1967* (Cambridge: Oxford University Press, 1968), pp.1-2.

16. *Ibid.*, p. 2.

17. See, for example, Jacques Chonchol, *El Desarrollo de America Latina y la Reforma Agraria* (Santiago: Editorial del Pacifico, S.A., 1964); and Julio Silva Solar and Jacques Chonchol, *El Desarrollo de la Nueva Sociedad en America Latina* (Santiago: Editorial Universitaria, S.A., 1965).

18. Roger Vekemans, a Belgian Jesuit, lived many years in Santiago and founded Centro Bellarmino, DESAL, and other organizations. He left Chile, voluntarily, shortly after Allende's election and now continues his work in Bogota. For a sample of his thought, see Roger Vekemans, S.J., *Çaesar and God—the Priest and Politics* (Maryknoll, N.Y.: Orbis Books, 1972).

19. The remarkable odysseys of the Chilean Christians for Socialism and the political philosophy of their main spokesman, Gonzalo Arroyo, S.J., have been ably documented in *Christians and Socialism: Documentation of the Christians for Socialism Movement in Latin America*, ed. John Eagleson, trans. John Drury (Maryknoll, N.Y.: Orbis Books, 1974).

20. Gabriel Bowe, *The Third Horseman, A Study of World Poverty and Hunger* (Dayton, Ohio: Pflaum Press, 1967).

21. See "L'accueil mondial à Populorum Progressio," *Développement et Civilisations*, no. 30 (June 1967).

22. See especially Jan Tinbergen, *Development Planning* (New York: McGraw Hill, 1967), chap. 3; and "Wanted: A World Development Plan," *International Organization*, ed. Richard N. Gardner and Max F. Millikan, 22, no. 1 (Winter 1969): 417-431.

23. Jacques Austruy, *L'Islam Face au Développement Economique* (Paris: Les Editions Ouvrières, 1961). See also, *idem, Le Scandale du Développement* (Paris: Marcel Rivière, 1965); and *idem, Le Prince et le Patron* (Paris: Editions Cujas, 1972).

Chapter V

MAKERS OF HISTORY
OR WITNESSES
TO TRANSCENDENCE?

Today's Christians have no choice but to take history seriously. Their own theologians—Dietrich Bonhoeffer, Pierre Teilhard de Chardin, Josef Hromadka, Gustavo Gutierrez, Harvey Cox, Rubem Alves, Johannes Metz, and others—have discredited the God who serves as a crutch for human deficiencies. None of the vital challenges posed by emerging social forces—world underdevelopment, the spread of mass technology, and new demands for total human liberation—can be met by postulating answers in "the next world." At their ordination, Christian ministers have traditionally recited Psalm 15: "The Lord is my allotted portion of the heritage, He is my cup." Nowadays, however, even priests and bishops know that it is this world with its problems which is their inheritance. They are conscious of betraying the gospel if they do not put their shoulders to the task of building history.

But can one labor at historical tasks with full

commitment while remaining (or becoming) a religious being? Leszek Kolakowski quite rightly asserts that there exist some "acts which are either performed completely or not at all. We cannot partially jump from a speeding train, partially marry, partially join an organization, or partially die. Accepting the world is one of those acts which cannot be performed partially."[1] So is it possible to keep faith with a transcendent God, who lies beyond history even though he acts within it, without deluding oneself or conniving with the structures of evil which still triumph scandalously in the here and now? "Religion is the opium of the people," taunted Marx a century ago; and Nietzsche said, Christianity is simply "a platonism for the people." These jeers still reverberate in the consciences of troubled Christians; they fear there is truth in them. Yet if Christians forego metahistorical transcendence, do they not thereby betray religion? Marx and Engels expressed the dilemma perfectly when they wrote of "a theologian who constantly gives a human interpretation to religious ideas and thereby constantly repudiates his fundamental assumption, the superhuman character of religion."[2]

In the field of development, this is one of the most agonizing tensions Christians face. How can they be present to history without abdicating their specific witness to a transcendent absolute beyond history? French theologian René Voillaume describes

the temptation for the Christian to commit himself with his whole being to all sorts of scientific, economic, social and political activities, so as to bring Christian influence to bear on the structure of tomorrow's world, at the possible cost of reducing Christianity to being no more than the best solution to worldly problems, *de facto* if not *de jure*, and losing the sense of a spiritual kingdom, of the transcendent nature of Christ's mission, of worship, and of the divine supernatural destiny of all humanity.[3]

On the other horn of the dilemma, however, no committed Christian wants to be accused of noninvolvement in the struggle to liberate oppressed humanity. The warning issued by Teilhard de Chardin in 1916 still echoes:

> so long as the world appears to me merely as an opportunity for gaining merit, and not a "final work" to build up and bring to perfection, I shall be but one of the lukewarm, and judging me by my religion men will regard me as below standard, and a turncoat. And who would dare to say they were utterly wrong?[4]

To combat underdevelopment, injustice, and exploitation in this world is not something one does because it is requisite to winning heaven, but because it is an urgent human task, worthwhile on its own merits. Christians, like others, need to be historical if they are to achieve their full humanity. The Uruguayan theologian Juan Segundo has written a comprehensive theological work in five volumes; the English series title is *A Theology for Artisans of a New Humanity*.[5] That is indeed the crucial question: *can* Christians be the artisans of a new humanity, the builders of a liberated human history?

I shall try to answer this question by separating it into four smaller questions, each of which encompasses an arena of conscience in which Christians face difficult historical decisions.

- Should one work at reforming institutions or at converting people?
- Is the way to liberation through class struggle or must Christians choose the way of reconciliation?
- Does Christian transcendence represent alienation from history or is it, rather, a summons to incarnate mystery within human history?
- What can Christians do to bring a "human face" to socialism?

Reform Insitutions or Convert People?

Sin is a central category for Christianity. It has two meanings: the whole human race's abiding tendency toward evil, and each person's inclination toward selfishness, manipulation of others, and ego-gratification. The message of Christian deliverance has traditionally been garbed in the language of freeing the individual from sin—greed, pride, lust, and sloth. From this emphasis, Christians have readily assumed that the conversion of individuals is a prerequisite of social improvement. By stressing the conversion of individuals, Christian apologists have, perhaps inadvertently, made people skeptical of the ability of institutions to produce greater justice. If one is convinced that human beings remain imperfect and subject to sin even after they have been regenerated by grace, he will not place great hope in the capacity of new structures or institutions to destroy exploitation. One question will always linger in his mind: what

ultimate good will new structures do, since
everyone is sinful and new forms of oppression will
inevitably spring up?

But sophisticated Christians are mindful of the
systemic impact of institutions on human
behavior. They understand that even the noblest
intentions of individuals cannot fully resist the
pressures wrought by pervasive cultural patterns
or neutralize the constraints imposed by imper-
sonal institutions. Accordingly, such Christians
are just as skeptical of the ability of "good people"
to produce justice as they are of the efficacy of
"just institutions." For this reason they reject the
conservative position that greater social justice
can come only from a moral rearmament of
individuals in society.

Their argument can be crudely expressed in the
following terms: making everyone good does not
necessarily result in a just society; conversely,
adopting good institutions does not guarantee
that a society will be just. The solution of this
dilemma must be to devise strategies for change
whereby efforts to improve individuals' moral
values can best support organized attempts to
modify imperfect institutions. Christians cannot
resolve this dilemma unless they believe—at least
implicitly—that men are able to forge institutions
which are morally better than themselves. Such
a belief underlies Christian acceptance of the
priesthood: men can be ministers of God's grace
even if their personal lives are not virtuous. In
the political order, adherents of democracy make
parallel assumptions: the role of judge and jury-
man can force an individual to rise above his passions, and constitutional guarantees are a better

safeguard of rights than reliance on the honesty
and wisdom of rulers or magistrates. In a similar
vein, Marx noted that capitalists are exploitative
not because their hearts are sordid, but because
their positions compel them to pursue certain
interests. Leaders in modern Marxist societies,
such as China and Cuba, also recognize that the
creation of new moral values in what they call the
new man must accompany the implanting of new
institutions. Human beings are not by nature
inclined to place service to the community on a
higher priority scale than self-aggrandizement or
private gain. Hence the need for constant group
criticism, for revolutionary committees to keep
vigil over the moral purity of revolutionary cadres,
for a punitive system which imposes harsh sanc-
tions on so-called crimes against socialist property.
It is ironic to learn that in "advanced" socialist
societies, such as the Soviet Union, theft or malin-
gering are punished very severely. Such punish-
ments seem a reversion to the primitive ages of
capitalism. During the Industrial Revolution, England punished crimes against property by sending
culprits to the gallows, and seventeenth-century
French clothiers resisted the introduction of modern printed calicoes by the death penalty. "In Val-
ence alone on one occasion 77 persons are sen-
tenced to be hanged, 58 broken on the wheel, 631
sent to the galleys, and one lone and lucky
individual set free for the crime of dealing in forbid-
den calico wares."[6]

But acquisitive instincts are not easily uprooted,
even when the overall structures of a society are
tailored to confer prestige and position on those
who serve the common welfare. Consequently,
those who believe in the permanence of sin find

empirical support for their skepticism *vis-à-vis* institutions in historical experience. Nevertheless, progressive Christians today flatly oppose their conservative fellow-believers who use this historical support as an excuse for approving the institutional status quo. The progressives agree with Kolakowski that the conservative

> constantly oscillates between the claim that the world is so perfect that it requires no change and the thought that it is so rotten that it defies change. It is not important which of these ideas predominates, because they both have the same consequences in practice.... He does not mean to say that the world contains no positive values but only that they have all been realized. He uses his conviction that the world is somehow "frozen" in its crippled state to protest against all reform; for he thinks this evil world is not only the best of all possible worlds but that it has realized its highest values....
>
> The conservatives, like the authors of earlier theodicies, are certain that all good has been realized in the world; that while evil is indeed evil, it cannot be eliminated, and each change that takes place is a change for the worse.[7]

The complicity with present evils that is born of inertia is what progressive Christians fight to overcome. Yet their task is not an easy one, since they, too, know that sin will continue and that even new structures and social systems can never, by themselves, abolish the possibility of evil. In Camus' words:

> Revolution, in order to be creative, cannot do without either a moral or a metaphysical rule to balance the insanity of history. Undoubtedly, it has nothing but

scorn for the formal and mystifying morality to be found in bourgeois society. But its folly has been to extend this scorn to every moral demand.[8]

Therefore, even revolutionary Christians are less sanguine than most Marxists as to the likelihood that new relations of production will destroy all alienation. Christians continue to believe that, at the deepest level, alienation means the sinful self-isolation of the human ego from divinizing influences which are proferred, but never imposed, by God. Human beings must be converted, even if their institutions are good, to prevent their reverting to the vilest forms of oppression or mystification.

Even theologians of liberation aspire after grace. Gustavo Gutierrez reminds us, in a recent essay:

> Jesus is opposed to all politico-religious messianism which does not respect either the depth of the religious realm or the autonomy of political action. Messianism can be efficacious in the short run, but the ambiguities and confusions which it entails frustrate the ends it attempts to accomplish.[9]

In other words, Christians can never place unbridled hope in the reform of institutions. Even when they accept class struggle as necessary, they must have no illusions that the proletariat has been vested, in any absolute sense, with the historic mission of redeeming humanity. The proletariat is also heir to human passions and vices. Because faith summons Christians to refuse to make idols of anything other than God himself, they cannot accept, in unqualified terms, the notion that any social class is the messiah of all mankind. Marx's claim that the oppressed classes carry *universal* hu-

man values within themselves is ambiguous. To
the extent that these classes are oppressed, nega-
tively speaking, his statement is true. But to the
degree that the proletariat asserts itself positively
by concrete historical choices, its members cannot
incarnate universal human values. Like members
of any other class, they are particularistic, they
are able to exploit others, they can get carried
away by their own self-conferred grandeur. Marx's
image of the proletariat is very romantic at root.
He almost sounds like one of the nineteenth-
century Russians Solzhenitsyn decribes, a man
who had "to change his clothes and feel his way
down the staircase to go to the people."[10] But those
who are themselves members of the proletariat
do not idealize the companions who share their
misery: like all men or women, they can be selfish
or stupid, lazy or aggressive, bitter or treacherous.

From this observation conservatives draw the
conclusion that government can safely be placed
only in the hands of qualified elites. But critical
Marxists and revolutionary Christians conclude,
instead, that even the people must have institutional barriers to prevent them from lording it over
others once they accede to power.

Inherent in Christianity is the belief that no one
can ever be fully converted to goodness. As Claudel
once put it facetiously, "There are parts of me
which have not yet been evangelized!" Nevertheless, the evil which a person commits is not irrever-
sible, and it can be minimized. Above all, it is worth
the effort to struggle to eliminate it. Hence the
question, "Is it better to work at converting people
or at changing institutions?" can only be answered

by saying, "One must do both." Christian progressives, like Marxists, give priority to altering oppressive institutions, without neglecting to emphasize the essential corruptibility of men, even in socialist institutions. They acknowledge that socialism can generate its own special forms of alienation. Yet, on balance, they prefer to run this risk than to support an oppressive status quo. The only alternatives they rule out are passive complicity with present injustice and a naive belief in the redemptive power of liberating institutions. In a critical spirit, they see liberation as a dialectical task: an endless process whose gains are always fragile, but whose promise justifies all sacrifices.

These Christian "makers of history" have an uphill battle to wage against the distrust of institutions innate in their acceptance of sin being firmly rooted in human life. One is not surprised, therefore, when some theologians of liberation seem to fall into a simplistic Rousseauism as they preach the merits of new institutions. It is as though they naively believed that men wielding power in those institutions could not err or could no longer be seduced by temptations to private wealth or ego-satisfying power over others. In most cases, however, such language is mere rhetorical overkill. Many use it because they deem it necessary to refute the abiding conservative bias of the traditional Christian insistence on human sinfulness.

There are further tensions faced by Christian moralists as they reflect on the development debate. Many progressive Christians feel uneasy over what appears to be the logical outcome of the Marxist tendency to deemphasize sinfulness and to emphasize liberating structures. New interpretations of biblical original sin will doubtless become necessary. Perhaps Adam's sin was hubris only in the sense that he did not recognize the perfections he enjoyed as gifts. Instead, he clung to them as coming from himself. Accordingly, he could view the "knowledge of good and evil" which the tempter placed before his eyes under two aspects: as a missing perfection he must have (since all perfection must be his); and as evidence that God had "cheated" him by denying him something valuable, to wit, full knowledge. As it turned out, "knowledge of good and evil" was not a further cognitive perfection, but the *experience of misery*.

At the cosmic level, the human race rightly aspires after its own redemption. And such redemption *must come in time, it must come within history*. Any redemption which is outside time, therefore, is alienating to men. But perhaps the human race, like Adam, is summoned by destiny to display a modicum of ontological humility, to recognize its finiteness by admitting that perhaps it may be radically unable to achieve total redemption in time. If the human race collectively interprets this radical impotence as an unjust deprivation of its due by jealous gods or absurd existential forces, it will reject any form of transcendence which would keep history open to fulfillment partially outside history. For mankind, therefore, to erect its own historical efforts as an absolute idol constitutes collective hubris analogous to Adam's personal sin.

Revolutionary Christians fully committed to history are beginning to sense that they may need to reinterpret their theology of history in some such light. They are encouraged by the pleas of such heretical Marxists as Ernst Bloch, Ernst Fischer, Leszek Kolakowski, and Roger Garaudy to help them incorporate even transhistorical transcendence into the human struggle. Garaudy's reflections are especially germane here. He declares that "Christians do not know how to live in a revolution," and explains that sin is not the revolt against authority, or pride, but the failure to fight against injustice, the "desertion of the creative human task." Nevertheless, he adds, Christians have two tasks: to contribute their resources of faith and vision to the transformation of this world so as to fulfill human beings; and "never to forget to ordain this renovation of life on earth to a finality which is ever higher. Faith, in this perspective, is no longer an opium, but the ferment of the continuous creation of the world by man, and the opening of human history onto an horizon that has no end."[11]

Hugo Assmann, a Brazilian theologian and sociologist, outlines the possible Christian contribution to liberation in even more precise terms:

It is clear that a rereading of the Bible, especially of the words of Christ, in the context of history raises for us a series of radical questions to which Marxism is unable to give the necessary attention. Perhaps the culmination of these questions is the Christian affirmation about conquering death, that radical alienation about whose overcoming Marx had nothing important or satisfactory to say.

The historical aspect of the problem of death is not the affirmation of our faith in a "hereafter" (which, as we know, does not eliminate temptations to egotism), but rather this: that the God who raised up

Jesus is not a God of the Dead but of the living and that because life is the "milieu" of God he wants it to be also the "environment" of men. When we understand this in a historical and trans-historical way, in terms of a Christian eschatology whose ultimate questions are necessarily mediated to us through questions posed by our immediate situation in history, we are able to penetrate to the heart of that mystery of love which is giving one's life for others. Marxism in fact asks the same of all revolutionaries.[12]

Christians have no trouble agreeing that the greatest sin today is omission: absenteeism from the liberating struggle. Yet liberation itself must be given its full dimensions; it cannot be enclosed within purely finite borders.

Class Struggle or Christian Reconciliation?

The divisions wrought by class struggle in societies at large have now made their way into the very entrails of churches throughout the world. On the right we find those who appeal to the classic Christian position of preaching reconciliation. They advocate that the church not take sides with the poor *against* the rich, and not become the unconditional ally of the oppressed *against* groups which oppress them. Their governing premise is that Christ came to save everyone: slaves and freemen, the rich and the poor, the mighty and the powerless. The church, they argue, is to stand as a witness to the reconciling powers of God's grace. Therefore, it is justified in exhorting the rich and powerful to pay heed to the demands of the underclasses and simultaneously appealing to the latter to adopt solutions which will not totally rupture the fabric of the Christian community. Under this argument, pastors and ministers of the gospel, in particular, must guard against lining up with any single faction of the Christian flock. Advocates of this position point to events in Jesus' life when he befriended the wealthy or powerful and to occasions when he refused to engage in purely political action even on behalf of Judea, then occupied by the invading Romans.

Many authoritative church documents warn against a diagnosis of social evils founded on class struggle. For example, in the opening paragraph of his encyclical *Populorum Progressio*, issued in 1967, Paul VI declared that the Church is at the service of all and that it is her duty "to convince them that solidarity in action at this turning point in history is a matter of urgency." Moreover, describing conditions of extreme oppression, he stated that "recourse to violence, as a means to right these wrongs to human dignity, is a grave temptation." Nevertheless, the pope acknowledged that a revolutionary uprising might be justified in exceptional cases "where there is manifest, long-standing tyranny which would do great damage to fundamental personal rights and dangerous harm to the common good of the country." But his main admonition was to avoid revolution, a course which, he said, "produces new injustices, throws more elements out of balance and brings on new disasters."[13] The pope revealed the true cast of his thought on this matter in Bogota, in 1968. François Houtart and André Rousseau reported:

[He] categorically rejects violent revolution as a means of creating a new society. He rejects it as "contrary to the Christian spirit.... Violence is not evangelical, it is not Christian." He also rejects it as odious because it entails want and ruin and "civil and religious decadence," and because it inevitably ends in a "burdensome dictatorship." And finally he rejects it as inefficient: "Sudden and violent changes of structure would be deceptive, inefficient of themselves."[14]

Later in the encyclical, Paul VI urged rich nations to place their superfluous wealth at the service of poor nations. He also called for improved planning and for a new kind of world fund drawn from monies previously spent on armaments. But above all, he pleaded for "dialogue between those who contribute wealth and those who benefit from it." Development is the new name for peace and must be achieved by the common efforts of all. His final exhortation reminded us that "at stake are the peace of the world and the future of civilisation. It is time for all men and all peoples to face up to their responsibilities."[15]

The Conference on World Cooperation for Development, sponsored by the World Council of Churches and the Pontifical Commission for Justice and Peace in Beirut in April 1968, made a similar prescription:

There can be non-violent revolutions. All our efforts must be directed to change without violence. But if injustice is so imbedded in the *status quo* and its supporters refuse to permit change, then as a last resort men's conscience may lead them in full and clear-sighted responsibility without hate or rancour to engage in violent revolution. A heavy burden then rests on those who have resisted change.[16]

Here, as in the encyclical and other church documents, a pointed diagnosis in terms of structural exploitation is followed by recommendations that all nations and classes work together for a world of greater justice. The underlying assumption is that there are no irreducible antagonisms between the interests of the haves and those of the have-nots.

Many radical Christian groups, however, accept class struggle both as an undeniable fact and as a starting point for devising strategies of change. For them, class struggle is the present historical context within which they must labor for both social justice and, ultimately, Christian reconciliation. To abstain from supporting the demands of the oppressed, they argue, is tantamount to taking sides with their oppressors. They believe that in Latin America, the only Third World continent where Christians constitute a majority and where their religion exercises a deep cultural and political influence a strategic alliance between revolutionary Christians and Marxists is necessary in the process of liberating the masses. Class struggle, they contend, has already proceeded so far in Latin America that the only two options left are socialism or dependent capitalism with perpetual under-development. They do not take their acceptance of Marxian economic analysis to be a betrayal of their Christian faith; it is, rather, the pledge of their serious commitment to liberating struggle, even as they probe to discover nonalienating modes of belief and religious practice. Such effort toward a new religious praxis, they insist, is the only argument that can refute Marxist atheism. Their actions reiterate the theoretical statement made in 1967 by Czech theologian Josef Hromadka—atheism is not inherent to Marxism but is the result of its historical conditioning in nineteenth-century industrial Europe.[17] This hypothesis has, in effect, been adopted by revisionist or radical Marxist philosophers: Milan Machovek, Ernst Fischer, Adam Schaff, Ernst Bloch, and others.

More politically significant, however, is the active involvement of Latin American priests and ministers in the class struggle. One must assume that they continue to take their own Christianity seriously. How then do they reconcile their participation in class struggle with the ministry of Christian reconciliation? They answer, predictably, in *dialectical* terms. They judge reconciliation impossible under present conditions. Therefore, they have decided that they must work to change these conditions so that reciprocity may begin to reign. To preach reconciliation now, at a time when established structures support paternalism, privilege, and exploitation, is not only to commit vicious hypocrisy; it is also to place the church in a nonhistorical posture which can only benefit the status quo. Their goal is truly reconciliation, once basic justice has been achieved. But reconciliation is also a means, inasmuch as their struggle alongside the oppressed must be waged without any hatred, vindictiveness, or blind stereotyping of enemies as incapable of overcoming the class consciousness which makes oppressors of them.

No satisfactory resolution of the tensions between the desire to shoulder the full historical bur-

den of the class struggle and the wish to be faithful
to the demands of Christian reconciliation has yet
been achieved by Christians in the Third World.
The vocal presence of partisans of both positions
within the churches is itself a manifestation of a
larger class struggle whose outcome is still in
doubt. Neither party to the debate is free, of course,
to ignore totally the claims of the other. Indeed,
many of the church's faithful are themselves members of upper or middle classes. Therefore, even
the champions of the poor feel a need to gain entry
into the consciences of these groups and wean them
away from their class loyalties—this in the name
of the gospel. Conversely, reality forces the defenders of reconciliation to admit the validity of the
claims of the oppressed. Even cautious Christians,
such as Paul VI, occasionally find themselves in
the position of advocating revolutionary change.
The tragedy is that, as Houtart and Rousseau point
out,

> the lack of a sociopolitical analysis of the event leads,
> therefore, to results which are exactly the opposite
> of those intended. Having stated clear and precise
> principles, the pope, without intending to do so,
> upheld the position of the oppressor exactly as he
> did in Bogota, where his call for rapid social change
> was quite clear, but where all the strength of the
> principles was dissipated by his specific remarks
> about the pace of change and his appeals to the pa-
> tience of the poor and the generosity of the rich. . . . It
> is certainly true that the Christian tradition encour-
> ages a non-violent attitude. But when, in practice,
> the dominating powers use this language to maintain
> the status quo, then the affirmation of theoretical
> truth can very well lead to its opposite in practice.[18]

The opposite danger awaits those Christians whose zeal for rooting their commitment to the oppressed in the historical moment leads them to adopt the class struggle model either too absolutely or too uncritically. Thereby they risk identifying their church with a particular faction which is no less capable of using religion to its own ends than were the capitalists and imperialists of earlier ages. This is a risk which Christians for Socialism in Chile and elsewhere are quite willing to run.[19] As they see it, the only alternative is to abdicate their responsibility both for the oppressed masses and for the integrity of the Christian gospel. The Church, they say, must not be *for* the poor, but *of* the poor. It must incarnate their hopes of deliverance from misery and oppression by sharing in their struggle to achieve human dignity. This can be done only by opposing the exploiters in struggle. Christian socialists deeply believe that the cardinal-archbishop of Santiago spoke the literal truth in November 1970, when he said,"In socialism there are more evangelical values than in capitalism."[20]

Alienation from History or Incarnation?

The present phase of history is characterized as much by the conscious drive to redefine and achieve development as it is by large-scale technology, the existence of nuclear weapons, and the rapid secularization of all values. Christian ethics has responded to the emerging consciousness of the Third World by attempting to resituate itself in history.

No other category has more pervasively influ-

enced Christian ethical reflection, both at the
philosophical and the theological levels. Christians
are always trying to be present to history, to read
the signs of the times, and to make of their religion
a fully historical witness. Stripped of all its trappings, this exuberant concern for history really
means one thing. Christians seek to find in their
faith and religiosity a high coefficient of involvement in the tasks of history: to build up science,
to abolish want and war, to explore nature more
fully, to bring human potentialities to fruition.
They must, accordingly, interpret their God, their
ethics, and their hopes—especially their aspirations after immortality and eternity—in such a
way as to allow them to plunge fully into history.
How can they do so?

Before addressing myself to this crucial question, I should explain why the question itself is
relevant to development. The answer is not in high
theory or speculation but in the realm of politics.
The specific operative concept here is political
mobilization. What beliefs can serve as spring-
boards for eliciting from people the sacrifices they
must make to abolish poverty and to build social
systems which foster human dignity for all? Any
philosophy which treats the miseries of this life
as unimportant or as necessary preludes to felicity
hereafter enjoys a low mobilization potential. Its
coefficient of insertion into history is weak. Conversely, any belief about the ultimate meaning of
existence and historical destiny which links personal effort to collective struggle can have a high
coefficient of insertion into history. These compari-
sons are not purely speculative: indeed most
underdeveloped nations have populations for

whom religious explanations of life and death still carry great weight. Accordingly, it is relevant to inquire into their religion's coefficient of insertion into history if we are to assess their chances of developing successfully.

To conduct such an inquiry here is doubtless impossible. Nonetheless, it may be useful to indicate a few points at which competing interpretations of Christianity make a vital difference on the scale of political mobilization for development.

The two focal points in Christianity which affect the mobilization potential for development are the relationship between human effort and divine initiatives in history, and the precise content given to eschatological doctrines. I have discussed this issue at length elsewhere, and I shall not repeat my argument here.[21] Nevertheless, it is evident that Christians may walk two "ways of the spirit." In the first model, they downgrade earthly efforts, emphasizing renunciation or abstention in the name of some apocalyptical fulfillment which is located in some other realm of existence. The dominant idea is that God is the principal actor in history, and history is seen as a moral proving ground where each person establishes his or her fitness for heaven. Hope in a *parousia* of the Second Coming of Christ serves as further reinforcement of the stance which despises mundane activities.

A second "way of the spirit," however, leads Christians to a different definition of themselves relative to God's action in history and to the eschatological meaning of human destiny. They see God's action in history as mediated by their own commitments; what God accomplishes thus comes to be determined by what they themselves

do. Not that God is powerless without them, but
rather he has chosen to create human beings as
makers of their own history with full freedom
inherent in their individual and collective
destinies. As for the teleological dimensions of
Christianity—the Second Coming and the Last
Things—this view does not interpret the final
parousia as some gratuitous intervention on God's
part, as pulling the human race's chestnuts out
of the fire at the twenty-fifth hour. No, final
redemption is prepared by the human effort to
make the world more finished, more just, more
expressive of all men's capacities—for good as well
as for evil. Even in this perspective, it remains
true that eschatological grace transforms this
world, as the scriptures say, from a world of corrup-
tion into a world of glory. But this can take place
only if the collective human effort to prepare the
coming glory has already achieved a certain degree
of success. This vision is clearly historical and
evolutionary. Its chief exponent is Teilhard de
Chardin, for whom the God beyond history challenges men to plunge more deeply into history so
as to render it worthy of their God's action. For
Teilhard, faith and hope in redeeming grace are
arguments which buttress his human commitment
to the conquest of knowledge, to the creation of
esthetic beauty, and to the maturation of societal
evolution so as to advance the collective ascent
of the whole human race.

Other Christian scholars—Ricoeur, Gilson, Daw-
son, Maritain— have insisted on the need to accept
this life as itself constituting an ultimate end of
human efforts. It is not purely a means or a plat-

form that allows the chosen few or, as the case may be, the redeemed multitudes, to gain eternal life. Eternal life, whatever it may mean, ultimately begins within time. Otherwise it is sheer fantasy. Yet, although secular history is an ultimate end having its own self-justifying finalities, it is a *relative*, not an *absolute*, ultimate end. Within its own order —of time, of change, of evolution, of dialectical antagonisms—it stands as the last word. And if that word is unintelligible at the tribunal of *human* language, *human* justice, and *human* creation, then life is indeed an absurd joke or a cruel condemnation. Therefore, God's providence does not redeem massive evils such as war, genocide, failed lives, and that common annihilation we all face at death. These are historical experiences, and it is in history that the alienations they bring must be overcome. Nevertheless, it is the belief of Christians that history is not an absolute ultimate end. Human history does not exhaust the totality of being's mysterious possibilities. Hence, the cosmic order may not be the final All. The special mystery of human persons is that they can shatter the boundaries of their own cosmic destiny and gain access—provided they actively open themselves to full transcendence—to whatever possibilities might lie in other cosmic orders, in other realms of being. Teilhard gave poetic expression to this hope when he constrasted

the pantheist, the neo-pagan, and the neo-humanist or the neo-earthling with authentic Christian humanists. The former love the world in order to enjoy it; whereas the latter, *who do not love the world any less intensely*, do so in order to purify it ever more and draw from the world itself the energies they need to transcend it.[22]

He further explains that it is because Christians have "pre-adhered" to God that they can triumph not only *over* the world, but *in* the world.

I am reminded here of a statement I heard Roger Garaudy make at a public session of Marxist intellectuals in Paris in 1963. He summoned his fellow communists to open their minds to wider horizons because "our Marxist humanism would be severely truncated if it were not 'big' enough to make room for John of the Cross." At a time when many Christian theologians are eagerly jumping on the bandwagon of secularism, independent Marxist critics are issuing salutary reminders that history and secular tasks are neither gods nor idols. One betrays the cause of history by forgetting that what makes human history important is its unrelenting drive towards transcendence. Societies we too facilely label underdeveloped may yet have the last word; for them, life and death are mysteries into which members of society must be initiated, not mere incidents to be recorded. Christians must not allow guilt over their past flight from history beguile them into rejecting that very transcendence which liberated Marxists and critical secularists are now discovering as genuine concerns.

The dialectic of existence is served neither by reductionist secularism nor by alienating supernaturality, but by the living tension in which human beings, as Teilhard tells us, find an issue or a way out of the impasses attaching to their finiteness and contingency. Therefore, Christians may be full partners in the construction of history even as they witness to the transcendence without which their hope is empty self-delusion. Che Guevara urged Christians to join the revolution "without the pretension of evangelizing the Marxists and without the cowardice of hiding their faith in order to assimilate themselves."[23] A century ago Marx and Engels had written that the proletariat

> cannot emancipate itself without transcending the conditions of its own life. It cannot transcend the condition of its own life without transcending *all* the inhuman conditions of present society which are summed up in its own situation.[24]

Critical neo-Marxists like Schaff or Fischer now acknowledge that death is a true alienation, not merely a natural necessity. Consequently, they too are now raising the Christian question: "Death, where is thy sting? Death, where is thy victory?" Nowadays, the question applies to the human race as a whole no less than to each person within it. Nuclear annihilation as a real possibility makes of eschatology itself a historical category.

The "Human Face" of Socialism

Few examples have been so rich in lessons for Christians as the public stances taken recently by the Chilean Christians for Socialism and by the Argentine Priests for the Third World.[25] History, these movements tell us, summons Christians to work with all their energies to build socialism. They do not judge their Christianity to be superfluous or inhibiting to the process. On the contrary, blest aspiration is to help build socialism 'human face." What precisely does this ion mean, and how does it affect Christians' on of their role in development struggles?

Christians for Socialism take Che Guevara's admonition seriously and make no effort to dissimulate their Christianity or to water it down. They agree with him that on the day "when Christians dare to give an integral revolutionary testimony, the Latin American revolution will be invincible."[26] To give such witness, however, they themselves must help build socialism. In no circumstances are Christians justified in standing outside their society's real historical choices, waiting for some pure and perfect system to appear. Socialism, as a historical force, represents the upward movement of organized societies away from the alienating contradictions of capitalism. Capitalism, even when it is smoothly adjusted to meet the demands of the welfare state, is essentially responsive to effective purchasing power. But in a world of mass poverty and unjust social structures, responding to purchasing power means giving the *wants* of the rich a higher priority than the *needs* of the poor. However, markets are not to be scorned, nor should efficient managerial practices or modern technology be rejected. Nevertheless, as Karl Mannheim pointed out twenty years ago, market competition and free enterprise assume a qualitatively different character according to whether they are the organizing principle of an economy or are used in subordinate fashion as regulatory mechanisms to control efficiency, waste, duplication, and assure flexible responsiveness to expressed needs.[27]

The Third World has been underdeveloped by

the dependencies bred by capitalism. Therefore, the political commitment of Christians to create a humane form of socialism represents a historically more advanced position than the vain search for some antiseptic third way or the timid abstentionism of those who fear repeating socialism's past errors. Here, I think, lies the crux of the problem. One must frankly admit that the socialist experiments already witnessed on the historical stage have largely betrayed their human charge of hope. The performance of socialist societies has not been equal to socialist theory. But this failure does not provide us with a worthy excuse for endorsing—actively or by default—a capitalism which, in its historical incarnations, has partly attenuated its evils in its matrix societies, thanks to the influence of other values. Like everyone else, Christians must assume their share of historical risks.

Do Christians fear that socialism must lead to a totalitarian political order? Let them heed their own Christian warnings against idolatry and deabsolutize the very political order they struggle to implant. Their religion forbids making an idol of any creature, and it commands them to guard the inner recesses of their conscience for God alone. Let them, therefore, frame laws where social privilege is strenuously extirpated whenever it reemerges. Thus can Christians help "humanize the face" of socialism—by first humanizing it within themselves.

In addition to combating political totalitarianism, Christians can contribute to socialist construction their unflinching insistence on the priceless value of each human person. For centuries they have had to reconcile the rights of personal conscience with the requirements of obedience to social authority. They should be well defended, therefore, against the temptation to *reduce* an individual's worth solely to his or her social utility. According to Christians, God loves each human being with a unique personal love. Believing this, Christian socialists can assert the primacy of personal worth in new communitarian modes. Thus will they incarnate, more historically than before, their own belief in the mystical body of Christ and the collective destiny of the fully redeemed (or liberated) human race. They must not become ashamed of giving primacy to love as a human category. Czech philosopher Milan Machovec, a Marxist, believes that

> man is a limited being, but in love and moral engagement he is able to transcend the limits of his individuality....I tend to think that genuine transcendence is the capacity for the "I" to seek out and find the "Thou."[28]

And Roger Garaudy pleads for an inward transformation of man and the creation of a new society in which love will become an objective reality of society rather than a mere prescription.[29]

Perhaps the central affirmation of Christians who labor to build a new world order based on solidarity and the repudiation of all alienating structures is that no person is bereft of moral grandeur simply because he or she is not socially useful or successful. The radical democracy of Christianity is founded on the individual's worth in the eyes of God. It is not the noble, the wise, or the successful of this world who will necessarily inherit the kingdom of heaven. This is a lesson to be kept in mind continually by Christian socialists no less than others. It is so easy for socialists to conclude that human greatness is ultimately to be measured in purely societal terms. But even a socialist saint is not necessarily the final paradigm of human success or merit. If this affirmation seems shocking, so be it: it is a constant Christian affirmation! It should leave even Christian militants for a new social order rather humble in their judgment of others. Ultimately, they cannot probe the inner depths of their neighbor's moral worth. Their greatest virtue, however, is not to use this disturbing Christian truth as an alibi for *laissez-faire* complicity with capitalism or as an excuse for their own tepidity in building history.

A third aspect to the Christian "face" of socialism is a liberating vision of material goods. What a paradox it is that modern Christians have needed the speeches of Mao Tse-tung to understand their own message of gospel poverty. According to Mao, economic austerity must not be seen primarily as a necessary evil to be borne by poor societies in the early phases of capital accumulation. The conventional view is that curbing one's desires for consumer goods and curtailing the production thereof are measures designed to increase savings and to channel more investment into productive facilities.

This will create a productive base from which an abundance of goods can be obtained in the future. Mao contends, on the contrary, that alienation through some future abundance presently desired is no less destructive of internal freedom and moral solidarity than alienation through an abundance already enjoyed. Hence, he concludes, austerity is a permanent component of authentic socialist humanism, not merely a necessary evil poor societies must tolerate in the early phases of development. No doubt production must be increased and new goods must become available to abolish malnutrition and to provide decent housing and sufficient clothing to all. But the first priority is to create a new consciousness in human beings, one not based on acquisitiveness at someone else's expense. Therefore, the austerity practiced today is a necessary moral support of one's social solidarity with all others. To be content with a modest sufficiency also provides one with a defense against the manipulative seductions of advertising or other devices aimed at multiplying wants. Moreover, an attitude of austerity reinforces the internal freedom of people engaged in herculean efforts at production; it guards them against the dangers of uncritically adopting technologies simply because they are efficient. Jacques Ellul's warning against the powerful tendency of technique to impose its own determinisms is taken seriously in China's development pedagogy.[30]

Anyone familiar with the tradition of gospel poverty will immediately note that Mao has understood the spritual dynamics of desire. Mao, like Christ, rejects both the puritan work ethic and the philosophy of resting content in one's misery. Gospel poverty is not a disdain for material goods but the refusal to let the desire for even necessary goods destroy one's spiritual freedom. In its full meaning, it presupposes a human level of want satisfaction in society at large. Jesus never praised poverty as a warrant to perpetuate inaction in the face of social injustice or rankly unequal distribution of wealth. Not by accident have Dorothy Day, Charles de Foucauld, and others discovered liberating joy in gospel poverty to the precise degree that they have fought unrelentingly against social privilege and the institutional idols of wealth and acquisition.

Perhaps the success of socialist endeavors in numerous societies outside China requires a new breed of Christians who will undertake living the beatitude of gospel poverty in order to protect socialist construction against the seductions of mass consumerism. For surely socialism can never have a "human face" if it endorses the notion that the fullness of good is synonymous with the abundance of goods. I have discussed elsewhere the difficulties entailed in sustaining the spirit of liberating poverty without a belief in religious transcendence.[31] What is germane to this discussion, however, is simply that Christian witnesses to the transcendent worth of gospel poverty can be effective makers of history in the mode of Mao's socialist humanism.

Conclusion

More clearly than ever before, we grasp how dialectical is the historical process. The struggles of secular makers of history have led them to reaffirm the need for transcendence. Their evolution is matched by that of Christian witnesses to transcendence whose own efforts at reinterpreting transcendence have led them to plunge ever more fully into the history that remains to be made. Paradoxes such as these are stumbling blocks only to those who have never understood that *yin* needs *yang*, that action demands passion, and that resistance to unjust structures requires contemplation. James Douglass gives eloquent expression to this mystery when he writes:

> If resistance is the yang of the Way of Liberation, then contemplation is its yin. The two are one, indivisible reality, and it is through them as one that the Way of Liberation is known.... As resistance seeks the social liberation of man from the pain of injustice, contemplation seeks his personal liberation from the pain of a deeper alienation, an impoverished and autonomous self. Man if liberated from his false self is united with the One, and personal separation and pain are overcome in the harmony of pure Being. Liberation understood thus in its contemplative form is an idea which pre-dates the liberation fronts of today's global revolution.[32]

The burdens assumed by those who would make history while bearing witness to transcendence become too heavy if their commitment is based on some rational calculus of probable success. That commitment can be founded only on a hope-laden calculus of possibility. One Christian advocate of renewed involvement in development, the Brazilian theologian Rubem Alves, has written a book called *A Theology of Human Hope*.[33] His title takes me full circle, back to the overall theme of this book: development ethics and liberation theology. Without an ethic of hope, the picture is bleak: there can be no genuine development or liberation for all. But hope, if translated into historical commitment, creates new possibilities. And it is always worth making sacrifices for the sake of the possible.

Notes

1. Leszek Kolakowski, "Ethics Without a Moral Code," *Triquarterly*, no. 22 (Fall 1971), p. 153.

2. Karl Marx, "The Holy Family," in *Writings of the Young Marx on Philosophy and Society*, ed. Lloyd D. Easton and Kurt H. Guddat (New York: Anchor Books, 1967), p. 363.

3. René Voillaume, *Au Coeur des Masses* (Paris: Cerf, 1965), p. 532.

4. Cited in Henri de Lubac, *La Pensée Religieuse du Père Teilhard de Chardin* (Paris: Aubier, 1962), p. 349.

5. Juan Luis Segundo, *A Theology for Artisans of a New Humanity* (Maryknoll, N.Y.: Orbis Books, 1972–). Vol. 1, *The Community Called Church* (1972); vol. 2, *Grace and the Human Condition* (1972); vol. 3, *Our Idea of God* (1974); vol. 4, *The Sacraments Today* (1974); vol. 5, *Evolution and Guilt* (forthcoming).

6. Robert L. Heilbroner, *The Worldly Philosophers* (New York: Simon & Schuster, 1966), p. 18.

7. Kolakowski, "Ethics Without a Moral Code," p. 158.

8. Albert Camus, *The Rebel* (New York: Vintage Books, 1956), p. 251.

9. Gustavo Gutierrez, "Jesus and the Political World," *Worldview* 15, no. 9 (September 1972): 44.

10. Alexander I. Solzhenitsyn, *The First Circle* (New York: Bantam Books, 1968), chap. 61.

11. Roger Garaudy, *Pour un Modèle Français du Socialisme* (Paris: Gallimard, 1968), pp. 371, 362, 372.

12. Hugo Assmann, "The Christian Contribution to the Liberation of Latin America," trans. Mrs. Paul Abrecht, mimeo. (Paper presented to Iglesia y Sociedad en America Latina, Naña, Peru, July 1971).

13. Pope Paul VI, *Populorum Progressio* (Encyclical issued 1967), para. 30-3l.

14. François Houtart and André Rousseau, *The Church and Revolution* (Maryknoll, N.Y.: Orbis Books, 1971), p. 216. The phrases in quotation marks are drawn from public statements made by the pope in Bogotá.

15. Pope Paul VI, *Populorum Progressio*, para. 49, 54.

16. World Council of Churches, Exploratory Committee on Society, Development and Peace, *World Development, Challenge to the Churches* (Geneva, 1968), p. 20.

17. See Marlène Tuinings, "Un lutteur paisible: Josef Hromadka," *Informations Catholiques Internationales*, no. 1 (November 1967), pp. 27–29.

18. Houtart and Rousseau, *The Church and Revolution*, p. 261.

19. See *Christians and Socialism* (Maryknoll, N.Y.: Orbis, 1974).

20. Cited in *ibid.*, Doc. 1.

21. See Denis A. Goulet, "Secular History and Teleology," *World Justice* 8, no. 1 (September 1966): 5–18.

22. Cited in Madeleine Barthelemy Madaule, "La Personne dans la Perspective Teilhardienne," *Essais sur Teilhard de Chardin* (Paris: Editions Fayard, 1962), p. 76.

23. Cited in "Both Marx and Jesus," *Time*, June 5, 1972, p. 57.

24. Marx, *Writings of the Young Marx*, p. 368.

25. On the Chileans, see chapter 4, n. 19. For the Argentine movement, see *Los Sacerdotes Para El Tercer Mundo y la Actualidad Nacional* (Buenos Aires: Ediciones la Rosa Blindada, 1973).

26. Cf. *Venceremos: The Speeches and Writings of Ernesto Che Guevara*, ed. John Gerassi (New York: Macmillan, 1968).

27. Karl Mannheim, *Freedom, Power and Democratic Planning* (London: Routledge and Kegan Paul, Ltd., 1951), p. 191.

28. Cited in Bernard Murchland, "Christianity and Communism: the Emerging Dialogue," *Worldview*, November 1969, p. 13.

29. *Ibid.*

30. I have derived my interpretation of Mao's advocacy of austerity from two sources. One is a series of comments made by Roger Garaudy in *Le Problème Chinois* (Paris: Seghers, 1967), pp. 224–227. The other is a conversation with Professor Paul Lin, a specialist in the Chinese Cultural Revolution. Garaudy has confirmed both that my interpretation of Mao is correct and that he disagrees with it.

31. Denis A. Goulet, "Voluntary Austerity: the Necèssary Art," *The Christian Century* 83, no. 23 (June 8, 1966): 748–752.

32. James W. Douglass, "The Yin-Yang of Resistance and Contemplation," *Freedom and Unfreedom in the Americas*, ed. Thomas E. Quigley (New York: IDOC Books, 1971), p. 112.

33. Rubem A. Alves, *A Theology of Human Hope* (New York: Corpus Books, 1969).